OPERATION TONGA

OPERATION TONGA
ELITE FORCES OPERATIONS SERIES – PARACHUTE REGIMENT

6th Airborne Division – June 1944

JON COOKSEY WITH TIM LYNCH

Pen & Sword
MILITARY

First published in Great Britain in 2023 by
Pen & Sword Military
An imprint of
Pen & Sword Books Ltd
Yorkshire – Philadelphia

ISBN 978 1 84415 203 2

A CIP catalogue record for this book is available from the British Library.

Typeset by Mac Style
Printed in the UK by CPI Group (UK) Ltd, Croydon, CR0 4YY.

MIX
Paper | Supporting responsible forestry
FSC® C013604

Pen & Sword Books Limited incorporates the imprints of Atlas, Archaeology, Aviation, Discovery, Family History, Fiction, History, Maritime, Military, Military Classics, Politics, Select, Transport, True Crime, Air World, Frontline Publishing, Leo Cooper, Remember When, Seaforth Publishing, The Praetorian Press, Wharncliffe Local History, Wharncliffe Transport, Wharncliffe True Crime, White Owl and After the Battle.

For a complete list of Pen & Sword titles please contact

PEN & SWORD BOOKS LIMITED
47 Church Street, Barnsley, South Yorkshire, S70 2AS, England
E-mail: enquiries@pen-and-sword.co.uk
Website: www.pen-and-sword.co.uk

Or

PEN AND SWORD BOOKS
1950 Lawrence Rd, Havertown, PA 19083, USA
E-mail: Uspen-and-sword@casematepublishers.com
Website: www.penandswordbooks.com

CONTENTS

ACKNOWLEDGEMENTS vi
INTRODUCTION vii

CHAPTER ONE THE PLAN 1

CHAPTER TWO THE MEN 10

CHAPTER THREE THE DEFENDERS 22

CHAPTER FOUR THE PREPARATIONS 26

CHAPTER FIVE READY TO GO 39

CHAPTER SIX PEGASUS BRIDGE 43

CHAPTER SEVEN THE MERVILLE BATTERY 56

CHAPTER EIGHT THE BRIDGES 62

CHAPTER NINE THE LANDING ZONES 69

CHAPTER TEN THE PERIMETER 72

CHAPTER ELEVEN EPILOGUE 77

ENDNOTES 79
APPENDIX I: ORDER OF BATTLE 81
APPENDIX II: OPERATION TITANIC 83
APPENDIX III: PEGASUS BRIDGE ASSAULT TEAMS 86
APPENDIX IV: OPERATIONAL ORDERS FOR THE PEGASUS BRIDGE ASSAULT 91
APPENDIX V: PEGASUS BRIDGE: A PERSONAL ACCOUNT 94
BIBLIOGRAPHY 97
INDEX 98

ACKNOWLEDGEMENTS

As a nervous newcomer to the field of military history, I approached Jon Cooksey with an idea for an article about a visit to the Falklands battlefields. As he did with so many others, Jon responded with the advice and encouragement I needed to get started and remained a reliable friend and mentor until his untimely death in June 2020. His teaching background and his passionate enthusiasm for history were evident to everyone who met him either through his books, his editorship of the Western Front Association's journal 'Stand-To!' or being guided by him on tour. This book is a reminder of how much I owe to him. He is greatly missed.

Thanks go to Dennis Edwards for permission to quote from his own account of his experiences at Pegasus Bridge and to the Glider Pilot Regimental Association. Thanks also to Matt Jones and the production team at Pen & Sword for putting it all together.

Tim Lynch
2023

INTRODUCTION

Normandy, 6 June: A line of jeeps cruises slowly down the road towards the bridge over the Orne Canal and parks outside the crowded Café Gondrée, their drivers relaxing in the warm sunshine. Across Normandy, the anniversary of the D-Day invasion is marked by fly-pasts, marches and parades to honour the dwindling number of veterans who return year after year. Schoolchildren learn directly from their grandparents and from the men who came to liberate their country what the cost of liberation really was. The names of their heroes are everywhere.

Above the hubbub, the skirl of bagpipes begins and people fall silent. A lone piper becomes the centre of attention, and around him old people pause in what they are doing and remember another time when they heard that sound. To them, it is the sound of freedom. Armed only with his pipes and a black dagger and wearing the same Cameron tartan kilt that his father had worn in the First World War, just after 1.00 pm on D-Day, 6 June 1944, 21-year-old Piper Bill Millin had marched proudly along this same road with his commander, Lord Lovat, leading the 1st Special Service Brigade up from SWORD Beach and across the Orne bridges to unite the airborne and seaborne invasion forces. The great gamble of Operation OVERLORD had paid off.

Almost as soon as the last boats had left the Dunkirk beaches almost exactly four years earlier, Prime Minister Winston Churchill had been looking for ways to strike back, forming Commando groups to raid the enemy coast and pouring resources into clandestine operations to 'set Europe ablaze'. Sooner or later, though, he knew that this would not be enough. At some point the British would need to take the war to continental Europe and this would mean landing a large force in France.

The entry of America into the war brought with it a new impetus. In the east, Russia was demanding that the western allies open a 'second front' to relieve pressure on their hard-pressed forces and a rally in Trafalgar Square supporting the call attracted 50,000 people. The newly-arrived Americans were keen to oblige with their plans for the immediate invasion of France under Operation SLEDGEHAMMER and unhappy with what seemed to them to be British reticence. Churchill argued forcibly that attacking head-on would be a mistake. Far better, he said, to strike the 'soft underbelly' via the Mediterranean. Only the failed Dieppe raid of 1942 finally convinced the Americans that an attack on Hitler's 'Fortress Europe' would not be an easy task.

In early 1943, the Allied heads of state met in the North African city of Casablanca to begin planning a large-scale invasion of France during the summer of 1944 and appointed a special staff group known as the Chief of Staff to the Supreme Allied Commander (COSSAC) to oversee the operation. In January 1944, just seventeen weeks before it was due to start, the proposals for an attack in Normandy were accepted.

Throughout late 1943 and into early 1944, COSSAC planners had considered the problems and the solutions to hundreds of scenarios and the thousands of logistical nightmares involved in massing, transporting, landing and supplying the 200,000 men in the first waves alone, and all in complete secrecy. Specially-trained divers swam ashore to collect sand samples from beaches along the northern French coastline – some risking their lives on beaches that were not even being considered – to maintain secrecy about the real targets. Logistics staff developed the extra-terrestrial-sounding PLUTO – Pipeline under the Ocean – to carry vital fuel supplies beneath the English Channel to storage tanks in France, while others designed and prepared pre-fabricated harbour walls ready to float across behind the invasion fleet. In France, resistance workers provided details of defences. Children playing in the streets and fields went home to draw the insignia they had seen around them and their parents eavesdropped on Germans drinking in bars. Every scrap of information would be needed.

It was clear to all – the Germans included – that an invasion was about to take place, but the question was where? Elaborate preparations in Scotland with radio vehicles driving across hundreds of miles of empty moorland to create the signals traffic of entire divisions made Norway a potential target. The building of fake landing craft, tanks and aircraft in Kent convinced the German high command that the Pas-de-Calais was the intended landing site. Captured German agents claimed it would be the Bay of Biscay on 15 June. On 2 June, cryptographers at the top-secret Bletchley Park facility decoded a high-level German signal. Initial attacks were expected in Normandy or Brittany, with the main effort to be launched later on the Pas-de-Calais. The deception had worked.

D-Day was to be a joint venture. American, British and Canadian troops would land on separate beaches and fight their own battles, eventually spreading out from their beachheads to link up and prepare to break out into France.

Every unit had its particular task, practised time and time again in the months leading up to June 1944. In the American sectors, US Rangers would scale the cliffs to silence the gun battery at the Pointe du Hoc overlooking OMAHA Beach. The 82nd and 101st Airborne divisions would drop to secure targets inland, including the vital raised causeways across the low-lying farmland behind UTAH Beach. The most important task of all, though, fell to the British and Canadian men of the British 6th Airborne. They would provide a screen on the eastern flank against the massed German forces awaiting landings on the Pas-de-Calais. They had to be prevented from reaching the invasion beaches, at all costs!

Airborne operations, by their very nature, are high-risk undertakings. The success of the 6th Airborne in preventing the German tanks smashing into the undefended flanks of the beach landings hinged almost entirely on the actions of a small group of men and six glider crews.

Just a few yards from where the modern-day jeep drivers sit and listen to the stirring sound of the pipes on the anniversary of D-Day – at the top of the road leading from the bridge to the nearby port of Ouistreham – is the very spot where all that planning, all that practice and all that preparation almost foundered and came to nought. In the early hours of 6 June 1944 a small German armoured reconnaissance force turned the corner, responding to reports of a landing by paratroopers at the Orne Canal bridge. A lightly-armed paratroop force could be easily dealt with by the local commander and his men began to probe forward. As they reached the junction, a single shot from a Projector, Infantry, Anti-Tank (PIAT) weapon stopped the lead vehicle dead in its tracks. Convinced now that this was a larger force than first thought, the tanks withdrew. A single shot from a notoriously unreliable weapon by Sergeant 'Wagger' Thornton had saved the entire British division from being cut off and destroyed.

It was one shot among millions and one decision among thousands, any one of which might have changed the course of history. With weather conditions against them, outnumbered and with no immediate support, the airborne assault could so easily have failed.

For the men landing in occupied Normandy in the darkness of that June night, however, failure was simply not an option.

CHAPTER ONE

THE PLAN

On 29 July 1944, Hitler awarded the Iron Cross to a 32-year-old Spanish businessman named Juan Pujol for his 'extraordinary services' to Germany. The news reached Pujol, head of a German spy network in England, by radio. He replied that he felt 'unworthy' and offered his 'humble thanks'. During the previous two years he and his team had supplied vital information to German Intelligence, broadcasting an average of four times each day in the first six months of 1944 alone with news of Allied troop and ship movements and earning a place as Germany's most trusted agent. In December 1944, he was awarded the MBE by the British government for precisely the same reason.

Pujol, or 'Garbo' as he was known to his MI6 handlers, was part of Operation FORTITUDE, a massive deception plan to convince the German high command that the Allied invasion of Normandy, when it came, was nothing more than a diversion to draw troops away from the Pas-de-Calais, already considered the most likely landing site by the Germans. Piece by piece, information was fed to German Intelligence about a fictitious First US Army Group (FUSAG) gathering in Kent and Essex in preparation for a cross-Channel dash. Dummy camps were erected, inflatable model tanks parked in fields to fool air reconnaissance, mobile wireless transmitters toured the countryside sending fake signals and all the while Garbo and others were sending their messages.[1]

In July 1940, Hitler had issued Directive No. 16 outlining his plans for Operation SEA LION, the invasion of England and specifically the use of artillery support. The plan called for the largest possible number of heavy artillery units to be placed so that they could be brought into effective action as speedily as possible to protect the flanks of the invasion fleet against naval counterattack by the British and to allow counter-battery fire to be directed against shore-based guns in England. Hitler demanded that the heaviest guns would be emplaced under concrete protection opposite the Straits of Dover so that they would be proof against even the heaviest air attacks. When the invasion was called off, those guns not transferred to the Russian front were given permanent concrete protection and, as the original directive had ordered, served to dominate shipping in the Channel. No longer able to support offensive operations, they became the first defensive elements of what became known as the Atlantic Wall of Hitler's 'Fortress Europe'. Later, his Directive No. 40 of 23 March 1942 ordered work to begin on an unbroken defensive line stretching from Norway to the Bay of Biscay.

The Führer's hero, Frederick the Great, had once written that 'he who defends everything defends nothing', but the enormous initial success of the

The Atlantic Wall defences of Festung Europa *(Fortress Europe). The German plan of defence rested on the ability of these fortifications to delay a landing long enough to allow armoured reinforcements to arrive.*

German forces had seen it conquer huge tracts of land across Europe which now needed to be held. In Russia, the German army held a front covering more than 2,000km; across the Mediterranean another 4,000km and from the Bay of Biscay to the Dutch coast it was held against the Anglo-American forces along 6,000km of coastline. Its best troops had been decimated in actions on the Russian front and reinforcements were increasingly difficult to find. From the protection of their concrete bunkers, it was believed that even a limited number of men could smash the Allies before they left the beaches. Initially, in August 1943, Allied planners had considered countering this logic by using airborne forces to land immediately ahead of the seaborne force to attack the defences from the rear. That plan had been dismissed. Experience to date had shown that parachute troops were too likely to be scattered and too lightly equipped to be of much use. Then, when Normandy was selected as the target, planners realized that the best of the German forces available were based east of the planned invasion beaches ready to move towards the expected landing areas along the Pas-de-Calais but still close enough to threaten the Normandy beachheads. A new role for the airborne forces was needed.

In an unobtrusive country house at Milston on the edge of Salisbury Plain between Netheravon and Bulford, staff of the 6th Airborne Division began their preparations. Security at 'Broadmoor', as it was code-named, was tight, 'almost too much so', as the divisional history recalls:

> *There was but a single key to the house and, when one day the officer who possessed it was delayed, he found on arrival a throng of eager*

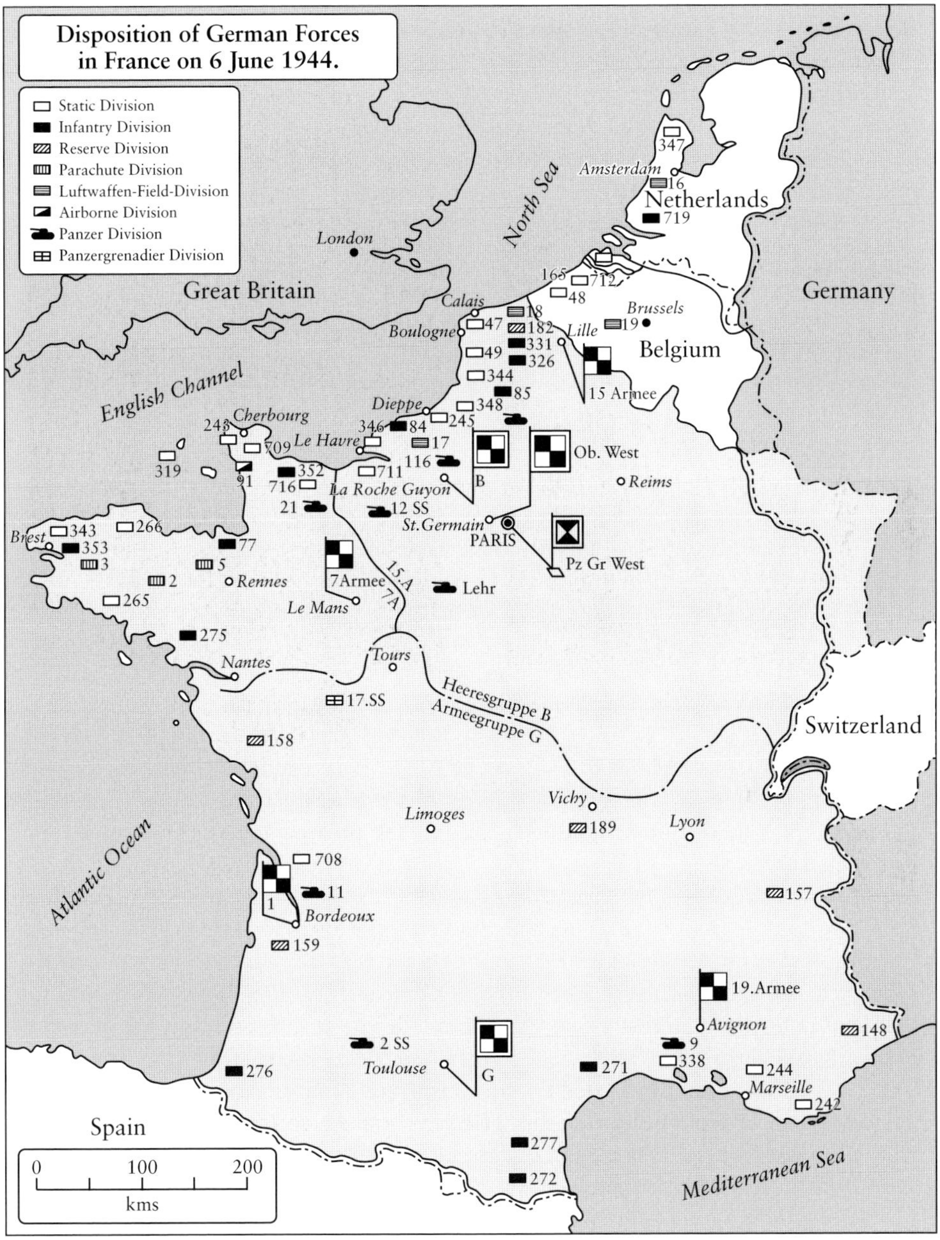

German deployment in France, June 1944.

planners, most of them of field rank, in a state of high indignation, for the door was fast locked and entry by any other means was impossible since all the windows were barred. For an hour the planners had had 'to fleet the time carelessly' in silence or in talk on more trivial matters, the nature of their occupation making it impossible for them to discuss what was uppermost in their minds outside in the churchyard which (ominously) stood next to the house.[2]

Here it was decided that the best use of the airborne forces in Operation NEPTUNE – the assault phase of the overall Operation OVERLORD invasion plan – was to throw a protective screen across the vulnerable eastern flank of the invasion, seizing the high ground overlooking the River Orne and to occupy, secure and hold a bridgehead linking them to the seaborne force. From there they would protect the landing on the beaches to buy time for the ships to unload their men and equipment and prevent the Germans from counterattacking from the east. With air-landing troops and paras in position, German reinforcements would be forced to divert south from the vulnerable flanks and would need to take the longer route towards Caen, with the result that they would have to engage the invasion force head-on.

Three key tasks were identified:

1. To seize the two vital bridges across the River Orne and Canal at Bénouville. Failure to secure these would result in the airborne troops east of the waterways being cut off from the seaborne force coming ashore later and trapped between the flooded areas of the twin waterways of the Orne and the River Dives to the east. A parachute landing was out of the question. The nearest drop zone was at Ranville and it would take too long to regroup and make it to the bridges before the garrisons set off the demolition charges already in place.

   In 1940 at the Albert Canal and again at Corinth in 1941, the Germans had used gliders to land forces directly beside the bridges, ready to fight as soon as their aircraft came to a stop. The year before, British gliders had attacked bridges in Sicily in the same way with limited success, but lessons had been learned. Men of the 2nd Oxfordshire and Buckinghamshire Light Infantry (2/OBLI) under Major John Howard would land in gliders and execute a *coup de main* operation to seize the bridges at the very start of the airborne assault.
2. To destroy the German heavy artillery battery at Merville, where reconnaissance indicated that there were guns capable of wreaking havoc among the ships of the invasion force offshore. The capture of the Merville Battery was assigned to 29-year-old Lieutenant Colonel Terence Otway and the men of the 9th Parachute Battalion (9 Para), and so vital was the mission that 750 men, one-tenth of the entire British airborne force tasked to Normandy, would be committed to it. It was, in effect, closely modelled on the German raid on the fortress of Ében-Émael on the first day of the war in the west. The main force of paratroopers would drop nearby and gather in a wood beside the battery to wait for the arrival of a force of sixty glider-borne troops armed with flame-throwers and explosives who would land in a precise attack inside the defensive perimeter. The task had to be accomplished by 0500 hrs. If no success signal was sent by that time, British ships off SWORD Beach would begin to fire onto the target, and any paras still in the area at that time would just have to take their chances.
3. To destroy the bridges across the River Dives. The low-lying areas nearby had already been deliberately flooded to hamper an airborne landing. The destruction of the bridges would make it an equally effective barrier to the German armour.

Paratroopers would drop to secure landing zones (LZs) and engineers would destroy the obstacles set up to prevent air landings in fields on the high ground above the Orne where gliders would bring in jeeps, trailers, anti-tank guns and other heavy equipment. Demolition parties would then be sent out to destroy a number of bridges nearby. Once secured and with the bridges demolished, the paras would withdraw into a defensive perimeter to await the arrival of the glider-borne Airlanding Brigade equipped with giant Hamilcar gliders carrying tanks. These would arrive as part of Operation MALLARD, which would begin on the evening of D-Day.

THE HAMILCAR GLIDER

GENERAL AIRCRAFT LIMITED (GAL. 49) HAMILCAR
Wingspan: 110ft
Length: 68.5ft
Weight total: 36,000lb; cargo: 17,500lb
Height: 20.3ft
Crew: Pilot and co-pilot
Loadings: Forty troops or one Tetrarch Mk IV (or M22 Locust) tank or two scout cars (or equivalent).
Tow speed: 150 mph
Glide ratio: 11.5
Towplanes: Halifax, Lancaster, Stirling.

Hamilcar glider silhouette.

First flown on 27 March 1942, the Hamilcar was the largest wooden aircraft built during the war, prompting the US army's glider procurement officer to call it 'the biggest hunk of airplane I have ever seen put together.' It featured a nose-opening door that opened automatically and could carry the Tetrarch or M22 Locust light tanks. These tanks started their engines during the approach and could be in action just fifteen seconds after landing, although there were incidents in which they started forward while still in flight and caused fatal crashes. A total of 412 aircraft were produced.

The dangers of airborne warfare: a crashed Hamilcar glider.

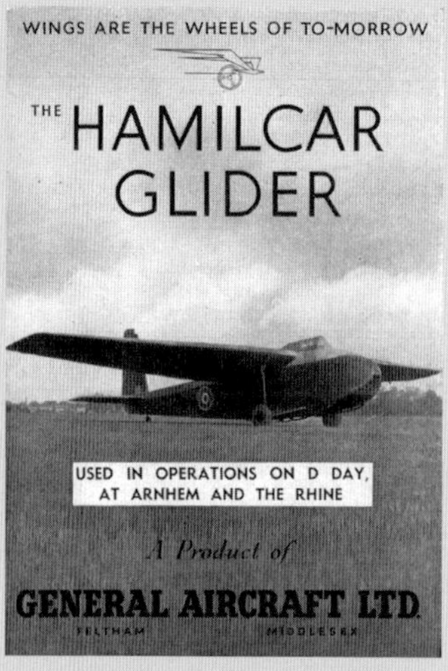

An advert for the Hamilcar glider.

A Tetrarch light tank loaded aboard a Hamilcar glider. On approach, the tank would start its engines and could be in action in just fifteen seconds. One danger was of the tank driver engaging the gears too early, which could send it forward through the nose of the aircraft, as happened occasionally with fatal results.

A Hamilcar on tow.

To do all this, the division would need to take, secure and control seven different landing sites designated either Landing Zones (LZs) or Drop Zones (DZs):

LZ 'X' and **LZ 'Y'** in the area between the River Orne and the Canal where D Company of the 2/OBLI and a platoon of the 249th Field Company, Royal Engineers would land by glider to seize the bridges over the Bénouville Canal and the River Orne in Ranville to prevent their destruction and to hold them until the relieving troops arrived.

DZ 'V' at Varaville would be under the control of 9/Para, tasked with the destruction of the Merville Battery, while the 1st Canadian Battalion engineers, dropping with them, would demolish the Varaville bridge over the River Divette and the Robehomme bridge over the River Dives.

DZ 'K' at Touffréville was the responsibility of the 8th Parachute Battalion (8/Para). Their engineers would destroy the bridges over the River Dives in Troarn and in Bures-sur-Dives.

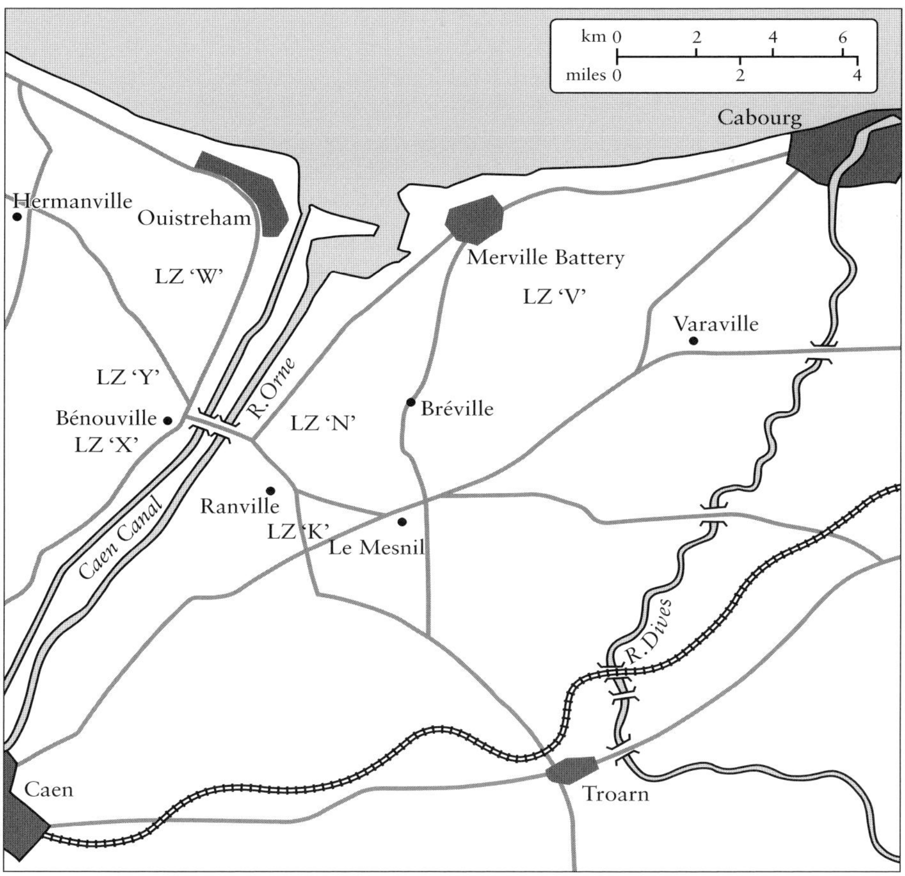

British Landing Zones. The grey area marks the high ground. The area to the right was heavily flooded.

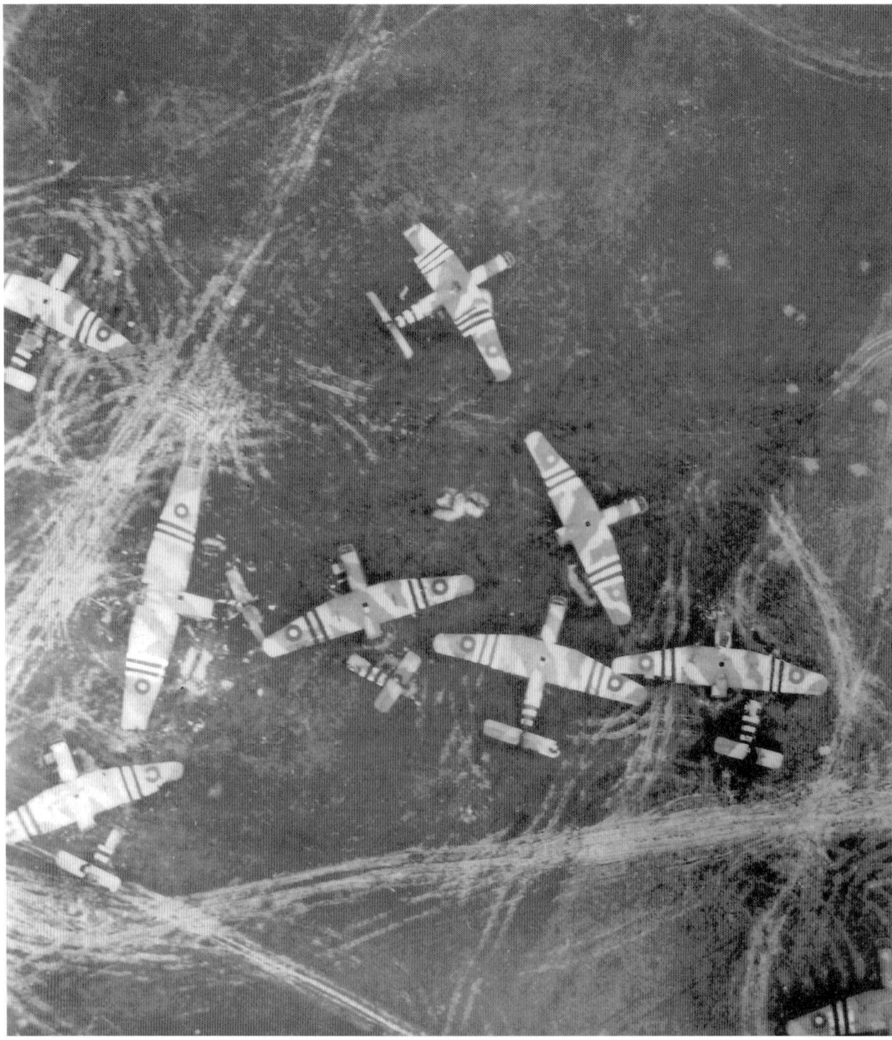

The difficulty of landing a fully-laden medium-sized aircraft is obvious in this shot of a glider LZ on D-Day. (Courtesy of Joe Larkin. Photograph taken by his father, Philip M. Larkin, Sgt./Photographer 30th Photographic Reconnaissance Squadron, United States Army Ninth Air Force on 7 June 1944)

DZ 'N' at Ranville would take the 7th, 12th and 13th Parachute battalions. Their mission would be to reinforce the Ox & Bucks men on the bridges over the River Orne and the Canal and to clear and secure the LZ 'N' for the gliders following behind. They would also establish a defensive zone on the southern flank.

LZ 'N' at Ranville would see the first wave of the gliders arrive at 0330 hrs and would be held to allow the landings of Operation MALLARD, with the resupply flights expected to arrive at 2100 hrs.

LZ 'W' at Saint-Aubin-d'Arquenay would be the landing zone for the gliders carrying 6 Airlanding Brigade and would form part of Operation MALLARD.

For the plan to work it would have to rely, as much as anything else, on the initiative of the men on the ground. Just before the operation got under way, Major General Richard Gale issued a general instruction to the officers of the 6th Airborne:

> *You must remember that it is your plan, and it must be your duty to ensure that it is your plan that is being carried out. Your responsibility in this is not one that you can be permitted to shirk. Your natural tendency may be to fight shy of it. You cannot; for ultimately the edifice is yours, and its foundation and cornerstones must be laid by you.... What you get by stealth and guts, you must hold with skill and determination.*[3]

Every detail had been meticulously planned, but every experience of the airborne forces to date had taught one thing above all. As 3 Para Brigade made its final preparations, its commander, 33-year-old Brigadier James Hill, was blunt: 'Gentlemen, in spite of your excellent orders and training, DO NOT BE DAUNTED IF CHAOS REIGNS. It undoubtedly will.'

CHAPTER TWO

THE MEN

Even before man had first managed to leave the ground successfully in hot air balloons, the use of air power in war was already being considered by men like Friar Joseph Galien (1699–1762) who, writing on aerodynamics at the University of Avignon, had speculated that once controlled flight had been achieved it should be possible to 'transport a whole army and all their munitions of war from place to place as desired.' In 1784, shortly after witnessing the ascent of the Charles hydrogen balloon in Paris, Benjamin Franklin wrote that

> *five thousand balloons, capable of raising two men each, could not cost more than five ships of the line; and where is the prince who can afford so to cover his country with troops for its defence, as that ten thousand men descending from the clouds might not in many places do an infinite deal of mischief before a force could be brought together to repel them?*

On 10 May 1940 German paratroopers began dropping across Belgium and Holland in a new form of warfare.

German paratroopers in action.

At 0430 on 10 May 1940, the nature of war changed forever when a force of eleven German Junkers Ju 52 transport planes took off from airfields near Cologne towing DFS 230 gliders, each carrying a force of specially-trained pioneer engineers. Their target was Ében-Émael, an underground fortress built in 1935 to guard the junction of the Albert Canal and the River Meuse near Liège in Belgium, a location that was vital to the success of the German blitzkrieg campaign, being the only point along the line of advance capable of withstanding the attack and delaying the invasion of Belgium. Planners had reckoned it could take weeks or even months to capture by conventional ground assault and that the ensuing casualties would be heavy. The German plan for the invasion in the west could not afford that kind of delay. For six months the special force had prepared, ready to be the first into action when the call came.[1]

Five minutes before the land assault was scheduled to strike into Belgium, the tow aircraft released their gliders high above the German border. Two immediately went astray, including that of the force commander *Leutnant* Rudolf Witzig. The remainder continued according to plan. Nine aircraft landed directly on the flat area on top of the fortress, achieving complete surprise. In Witzig's absence, Sergeant Major Wenzel immediately took command of the fifty-five men and began to eliminate the anti-aircraft defences and knocked out nine positions in just ten minutes. By the time Witzig caught up with his men three hours later they had control of the surface levels of the fort. Assault engineers then began to infiltrate the airshafts and tunnels to disable the gun casemates.

A force of paratroopers under Captain Koch had meanwhile landed by glider and seized control of three vital bridges nearby and by that afternoon ground forces crossed the frontier and reached the bridge parties. At a cost of 6 killed and 13 wounded, a force of 85 men had neutralized the strongest fortress in Europe,

On 10 May 1940, a small group of airborne troops landed on the roof of the supposedly impregnable Belgian fortress of Ében-Émael and captured it, opening the way for troops to cross into Belgium. Hitler personally awarded the Knight's Cross to the leaders of the attack.

killed 23 Belgians, wounded 59 more and rounded up around 700 prisoners of war. The capture of the bridges had opened the way for the Germans to overrun Belgium and to outflank the Anglo-French armies facing their Army Group 'A'. As the ground forces moved west, ahead of them across Holland German paratroopers were dropping into action and Ju 52s landed on roads, in fields, on beaches or anywhere troops were needed. The Germans seemed to be everywhere at once and resistance crumbled. The Dutch surrendered in days.

The stunning success of the German airborne operations sent shock waves through the Allied corridors of power. On 22 June, British Prime Minister Winston Churchill, always an eager supporter of unorthodox forces, sent a memo to his chief of staff declaring that

> *We ought to have a Corps of at least 5,000 parachute troops. I hear something is being done to form such a Corps but only on a small scale. Advantage must be taken of the summer to train these forces who can nonetheless play their part meanwhile as shock troops in Home Defence. Pray let me have a note from the War Office on the subject.*

Initially dismissed by many as simply another example of Churchillian folly – where, for example, were suitable aircraft to be found when the RAF was already stretched to its limit? – the idea itself was sound. German airborne tactics had already been highly effective when used in what Kurt Student – the commander of the German paratroopers, *Fallschirmjäger* – termed 'oil spot', dispersed attacks specifically

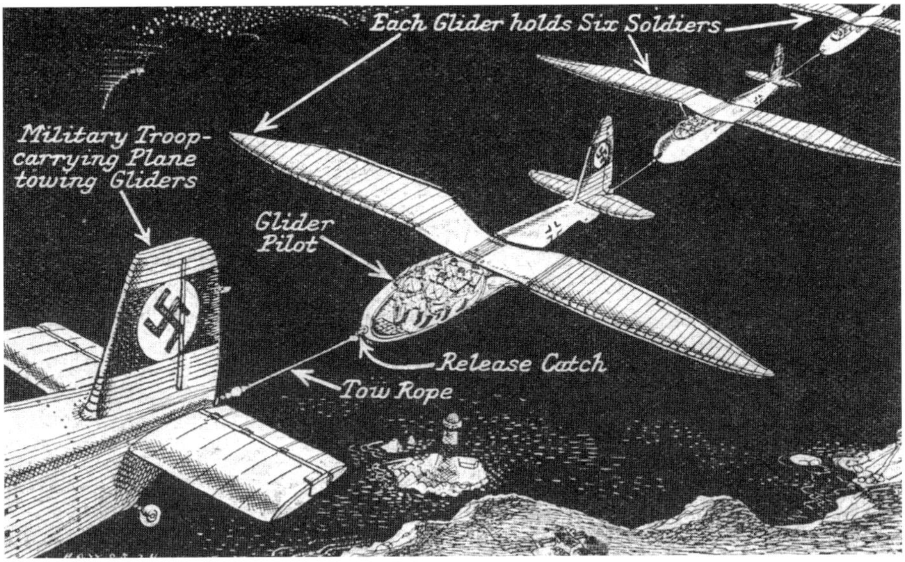

In Britain fear of an airborne attack was widespread and the public prepared for glider-borne and parachute attacks.

planned to confuse the enemy as to where the main assault would come. At the time of Churchill's request for information as to the progress of planning for a paratroop force, its conventional forces had lost heavily in terms of weapons and transport and its ability to respond to attack was limited. The swift use of airborne troops, should their use be developed, would allow for a rapid reaction force to support the spears and pitchforks of the Local Defence Volunteers (LDV) in containing any possible future German attacks before a viable airhead could be established.

In September 1918, US General William 'Billy' Mitchell had commanded a joint Franco-American force of almost 1,500 aircraft and frequently used 200 or more aircraft at a time for the mass bombing of enemy targets. Mitchell was an enthusiastic advocate of the view that air power was a vital element of warfare, a view he shared with his British counterpart Major General Hugh Trenchard. As the US First Army fought its way slowly through the Argonne Valley, losing 117,000 men in an advance of less than 32 miles, a young officer named Lewis H. Brereton proposed an audacious scheme to drop the US 1st Division by parachute from a force of Handley Page 0/400 bombers to capture the fortified city of Metz. This, he believed, would allow them to leapfrog the fierce German resistance, capture a major defensive position and at the same time cut the rail supply to the Germans by seizing the important rail junction in the city. Suitable parachutes were already available, having first been developed as fairground stunt attractions, but were now adapted for use by the crews of observation balloons who were, quite literally, sitting targets for German fighter planes. Although the British Air Board had refused their use by combat pilots, arguing that the provision of an escape mechanism 'invited cowardice in action' (an attitude that would cost around 6,000 lives before the order was overturned in September 1918), no barriers to their use by infantrymen could be found. Mitchell championed the idea, but it was halted by the American

Expeditionary Force's commander General 'Black Jack' Pershing and it would be almost twenty-six years before Brereton finally saw his 'plan' put into action as commander of the First Allied Airborne Army during Operation MARKET GARDEN in September 1944. In the years after the First World War, 'Billy' Mitchell's maverick ideas about the use of air power and 'vertical envelopment' by parachute troops would lead to his eventual court-martial and resignation from the army. He died in 1935, but was posthumously reinstated as a general in the United States army in 1946 after many of his theories had been proved effective in action.[2]

In the years following the First World War, neither Britain nor America saw any real use for parachute troops; nonetheless, training centres were established purely for the use of aircrews. Britain made a few tentative steps towards developing air-landing forces by taking delivery of the new twin-engined Vickers Vernon troop carrier in 1922 and using it to move troops rapidly into Iraq to capture dissident tribesmen. Ten years later, infantrymen of the 1st Northamptonshire Regiment were again airlifted into Iraq to quell another anti-British revolt. The American military considered parachuting to be little more than an entertaining diversion, but airlifted US Marines into Central and South America for small-scale policing missions. Some experiments were conducted in the use of parachutes for infantry purposes but, to use André Beaufre's memorable phrase, the Allies 'suffered a lot from victory'. Defence spending was low and public opinion strongly anti-military as nations struggled to cope with the massive losses incurred by more than four years of world war. Year upon year defence spending was cut to the point that by 1940 General Bernard Montgomery, then a divisional commander of the British Expeditionary Force in France, complained that some units were unfit to take part in even a realistic exercise, let alone a real shooting war. Sending men into combat, he claimed, 'would be sheer massacre'. Faced with financial constraints that prevented large-scale exercises in the late 1930s, the development of new and apparently fanciful units took very low priority.

Now, however, things had changed. Two days after Churchill's memo of June 1940, Major John F. Rock of the Royal Engineers was summoned to the War Office and put in command of Britain's airborne forces. How, with what and where were not explained. 'It was impossible,' he wrote in his diary, 'to get any information as to policy or task.' Rock's previous experience of aircraft was limited to having travelled as a passenger and he knew nothing of parachutes or gliders beyond what had appeared in the newspapers over the previous weeks as news of the German attacks on Holland filtered back. Nevertheless, he approached his task with enthusiasm and soon established himself at Ringway (now Manchester Airport) under its RAF Station Commander, Group Captain L.G. Harvey, assisted by Squadron Leader Louis Strange and Wing Commander Sir Nigel Norman where they set up the RAF Central Landing School. Starting, literally, at 'Rock bottom', the school's existence and purpose caused confusion within the bureaucracy of the War Office, and not least with the mail. In the early days a letter arrived for one recruit, Private Crane, addressed to the Central Sunday School, while a name change to the Central Landing Establishment (CLE) brought mail addressed to the Central Laundry Establishment! Slowly, though, the fledgling Army Air Corps began to spread its wings.[3]

Britain's fledgling airborne force began with the use of civilian gliders like this Kirby Kite, quickly repainted in camouflage colours.

The CLE evolved rapidly. A Development School was set up quickly to explore methods of using parachutes and containers to drop men and supplies, while the Parachute School under Group Captain Newnham, staffed by instructors drawn from the army and RAF – including, among others, a former 'Wall of Death' rider, a circus acrobat and a male ballet dancer – began its first experimental course on 13 July 1940. By 1944, the instructing staff had completed more than 16,000 jumps between them and all had taken part in operations.

Alongside the parachute school, a Glider Training Squadron was formed on 19 September 1940 using donated civilian Kirby Kite and other sailplanes, aging Avro 504 and Tiger Moth biplanes to tow them and civilian instructors. On 26 October, a demonstration took place using two tug and sailplane combinations and, almost immediately, the Ministry of Aircraft Production issued specifications for an eight-seat assault and training glider. Within four months, General Aircraft Limited (GAL) had successfully flown the GAL 48 Hotspur Mk I and an order was placed for 400 of them.

On 3 December 1940, the first parachute exercise took place with 350 paratroopers dropping on a foggy morning from four converted Whitley bombers. Only one casualty was sustained in the drop and the men set off for their objective, commandeering the car of Norway's Crown Prince Olaf on the way. By 28 February 1941, under the headline 'Not All the Parachutists Are Nazis!', *The War Illustrated* publication was able to report on a parachute raid against southern Italy by a force of British paratroopers. On 10 February, a team of seven officers and thirty-one men selected from a long list of volunteers at the CLE was dropped in a raid against the aqueduct close to Monte Vulture intended to disrupt water supplies to Italian operations in Albania. It was not a great success and all the raiders were captured, but it proved it could be done. Despite this, by April 1941 Churchill was becoming anxious about the airborne

The need for an assault glider led to the development of the eight-seat Hotspur. Although never used in combat, it remained the standard trainer for the Glider Pilot Regiment.

force and especially about the glider programme, asking 'Is it being seriously taken up?' So far, his glider force consisted of a single Hotspur delivered on 6 April and used a few days later and in a demonstration on the 26th consisting of a flypast of the Hotspur alongside five Kirby Kites in camouflage paint. This was followed by a planned drop of forty paratroops (of whom six failed to jump) which did little to inspire him, although he liked the newly-designed airborne dagger presented to him.

The first paratroopers were intended to work as guerrillas and many of the early volunteers had fought in the Spanish Civil War on one side or the other. Troops consisted of fifty men – one captain, two subalterns and forty-seven others – and each troop commander was originally given a great deal of freedom in how his men were trained until a formal Airborne Forces School and Depot was established under Lieutenant Colonel Down. In Whitehall, the 'Dungeon Party' under First World War veteran Major General Frederick 'Boy' Browning, who had earned his nickname when he first joined his battalion of Grenadier Guards on the Western Front in 1915, worked in underground offices to develop an airborne doctrine, and two separate but mutually supporting forces grew. Brigadier Richard 'Windy' Gale – educated for a period in the same schoolroom as William Shakespeare in Stratford-upon-Avon – took command of 1 Parachute Brigade, responsible for the initial assault phase of an operation with lightly-armed paratroopers, while Brigadier George 'Hoppy' Hopkinson assumed control of 1 Airlanding Brigade, which would follow up with heavy equipment carried in gliders. Gradually, the 1st Airborne Division took shape. A raid against the German radar installation at Bruneval was a great success, and throughout 1942 the 'Red Devils' proved themselves in action in North Africa.

A demonstration drop at the Central Landing Establishment on 25 May 1941.

The King inspects men who would go on to form the Army Air Corps, 25 May 1941.

'A superb salesman': George Chatterton, commander of the Glider Pilot Regiment.

The main problem, as the Germans had already realized, was that of deploying the force in combat conditions and even today, under ideal conditions, a paratroop force needs at least fifteen minutes to regroup and become effective. At Ében-Émael and later at other targets, the attackers needed to be able to be in action much faster. Gliders provided the solution. They could land almost directly on top of a target and the troops could fight as soon as the aircraft came to a halt.

In Britain, work to develop glider operations had continued. John Rock – by now Lieutenant Colonel Rock – had become the commanding officer of the 1st Battalion, Glider Pilot Regiment (GPR) on 21 December 1940. As his second-in-command, Rock had been joined by a man who would become an airborne legend, Major George Chatterton. A former naval cadet at Pangbourne College and then an RAF pilot with 1 Squadron, Chatterton's flying career had ended prematurely in a crash in 1935. Most recently a veteran of France with the Queen's Royal Regiment, Chatterton had been recruited by General Browning and brought with him two Guards sergeant majors and a firm belief in discipline. It was his intention, in his own words, to be 'quite ruthless' in enforcing army standards. It was a source of friction between the two men that would last until Rock's death in a flying accident in October 1942 but which would, as Chatterton demanded, ensure that those who stayed the course were not simply men seeking to escape the boredom of garrison life by volunteering for anything but would be, as Jim Davies, an early volunteer, put it: 'men who would put up with anything for the sake of flying.'

Glider pilots in the British army were not simply pilots delivering troops. Ideally, they would land their cargos and return as quickly as possible to their bases ready to fly another glider, but Chatterton, described by one of his pilots as 'a super salesman who could sell you anything', persuaded Browning that the men of the GPR would not be glorified truck drivers. His aim was to create a force of 'total soldiers', able not only to fly their gliders into action but also to operate any weapons they carried aboard and to lead airborne troops into combat. One volunteer, Alexander Morrison, recalled Chatterton's opening address to a new group of hopeful recruits:

> *Please sit down. My name is George Chatterton and I am the Commanding Officer of the Glider Pilot Regiment. You are all volunteers and, at this moment in time, have no idea what you are letting yourselves in for! Well, the Glider Pilot Regiment is part of the Army Air Corps and will have the honour of delivering men, guns, vehicles and even tanks right into the heart of the forthcoming battle.... This, then, will be your job and in it, you will be unique because you will not only have to be a*

top-rate pilot, but also able to fight efficiently after landing. You will be taught to fly while, at the same time, mastering every type of weapon and vehicle. Associated with your training you must develop the highest form of personal discipline...you will find that the next few weeks will tax your strength and moral courage to the limit.[4]

Volunteers for the new force came forward in their thousands, but were weeded out by an RAF selection board using the same standards as would be applied to RAF aircrew and by a rigorous training schedule that would eventually see just one in twenty-five trainees achieve their 'wings'. Conditions at the GPR depot have been described by veterans as 'hostile' and some wondered whether they had mistakenly been sent to a penal unit. 'You had to be fanatical to stay there,' recalled John Potts. 'One chap showed up on parade with a small cut on his face and was put on a charge for being "idle while shaving"!' Legend has it that an entire parade jumped to attention when a dog barked, but it created a strong sense of confidence in the trainees and those who didn't like it were free to leave. Chatterton genuinely believed that such a regime was vital to developing the skills and discipline needed to carry out their tasks and, when staff at one RAF base appeared to be sneering at his trainees, he visited the station, flying in by Tiger Moth to land 'in the most split-arsed manner' and emerge in parade uniform with a swagger stick under his arm and RAF wings prominently displayed on his tunic.

Troops being introduced to the Horsa glider. Its plywood construction and its tendency to induce airsickness meant that even hardened paratroopers came to respect the 'glider riders'.

A failed first operation against the German heavy water production facility in Norway during 1942 was followed in 1943 by the disastrous invasion of Sicily. Eager to prove his theories of glider-borne warfare by ensuring that his 1 Airlanding Brigade took a prominent part in the planned attack, pre-war amateur pilot and gliding enthusiast 'Hoppy' Hopkinson lobbied Montgomery to argue forcefully for a role. Having secured agreement, Hopkinson returned to his headquarters a happy man, seemingly unconcerned that there was not one British glider available in the whole of North Africa to carry out the task. Both George Chatterton and his RAF colleague Nigel Norman had been summoned to a briefing on the upcoming operation, but Norman had been killed when the engines of the Hudson in which he was travelling failed soon after take-off in the UK. Chatterton, without his friend's support, listened in dismay as the plan was put to him. Not least of the problems, he argued, was finding the aircraft in the first place. Hopkinson dismissed his concerns, with the airy comment that 'the US Air Force is going to supply tugs and gliders'. For Chatterton, it was the final straw. A night landing in unknown terrain was bad enough, but doing it in a glider that the pilots had never even seen before was a recipe for disaster and he said so. However, Hopkinson was not one to accept criticism of his plan:

> *Now look here, Colonel Chatterton, I'm going to leave you for half an hour and in that time you can study the photographs (of the LZs in Sicily). If, at the end of that time, you still feel that this is too difficult for you, you can consider yourself relieved of your command.*

Chatterton was aware that technically, Hopkinson did not have the power to carry out his threat but that he could make life very difficult for him. Nothing he saw in the photographs encouraged him and he was left with the belief that the operation would be deadly for his crews, but he knew that to refuse would simply mean that someone else would be placed in charge of the glider-borne landings. There was no choice. When Hopkinson returned he said nothing, but the general's mood changed dramatically. As Chatterton wrote later, 'he was like a little boy. He was so pleased.'[5]

In the event, untrained US tow plane pilots, unnerved by the sight of flak over the island, released their gliders far out to sea and fled. Hopkinson was among those fished out of the water and Chatterton recalled seeing him later, looking chastened at the sight of the few wrecked gliders that had reached land. By the end of the first phase, eighty-eight British and thirteen US glider pilots were missing, presumed drowned. Back in North Africa, tempers were running high. General Sir John Hackett, then with the reserve brigade, wrote that

> *glider pilots who were recovered from the sea came back looking for tug pilots' throats to cut. I saw no option but to confine them to camp until after the American parade for the award of decorations for gallantry, by which time the admirable qualities always to be found in glider pilots had reasserted themselves and calm was restored.*

The second phase proved no better. Three days after the first wave, the next airborne element climbed into their aircraft and at first, all went well. The ships of the seaborne invasion fleet had been told of the routes and timings of the air fleet, but somewhere off Cape Passero some thirty aircraft strayed into the no-go zone established around the ships. Nervous gunners below opened up. Two aircraft were shot down immediately and another nine turned back because of damage and injuries.

Six more turned back, claiming they had been ordered to do so by their squadron commander. The firing had alerted the shore-based defenders and flak now added to the damage, another nine paratroop-carrying aircraft were shot down and three glider combinations went missing. Aboard one C-47, Lieutenant Colonel Pearson, commanding the 1st Battalion of the Parachute Regiment, noticed the glow of Mount Etna below. Realizing that they were off course, he jokingly asked one of his men, a former pilot, if he could fly the Dakota and was assured that the man could. Moving forward, Pearson told the pilot that they had overshot the DZ:

> *His co-pilot was sitting with his hands over his face, crying 'We can't, we can't.' 'Can't do what?' I said. 'We can't go in there.' I could see quite clearly blobs of fire. I knew what was going through his mind, and it was going through mine as well because on the ground were what I thought were burning Dakotas. I said to the pilot, 'There's nothing for it boy, we've got to do it. If your co-pilot's no good I've no hesitation in shooting him.' I pulled out my revolver. The pilot continued with his protests. So I said 'I could shoot you as well.' 'You can't do that; who'd fly the aeroplane?' I said, 'Don't worry about that, I've got a bloke in the back who can fly this.' 'Yeah, but he won't know how to land it!' 'No-one has asked him to land the bloody thing – you don't think he's going to hang about to land it, do you? He'll be stepping out very sharp!'*

Faced with the fact that none of their passengers expected to return with them to their base and that they were by now surplus to requirements, the pilots reluctantly headed back towards the DZ but dropped the paras too low and at too high a speed, causing a number of casualties as they hit the ground hard.[6]

Even as the Allied airborne force landed and began to regroup, German reinforcements began arriving by air from Italy in what would be the only time when both sides used airborne landings on the same target. In the confusion, on the DZ near the bridge a British soldier was approached by a shadowy figure asking '*Haben sie meine Schmeisser gesehen?*' ('Have you seen my Schmeisser?' [the MP40 submachine gun]). As the British para searched for his weapons bundle, the Germans still dropped separately. Over the next few days, paratrooper would fight paratrooper in a fierce contest.

The problems in Sicily were summed up in Staff Sergeant Galpin's laconic analysis of the operation in a comment only he, as the only man to actually reach his objective, could have made: 'My observations at the time were that the following points were of interest in planning future night operations.... Landing right on top of the objective is the best recipe for success.' With fifty-seven pilots dead and hundreds of their passengers lost at sea, the belief in a precision assault by glider had taken a sharp blow.

In England, Brigadier Gale had watched the progress of the operation in dismay. He had not been with the Parachute Brigade when it left for North Africa, instead remaining behind to further develop airborne doctrine. In May 1943 he had been promoted to major general and given command of Britain's second airborne division, designated the '6th Airborne' as a bluff to artificially inflate the size of the British parachute force. As the reports from Sicily came in, Gale took the news on the chin and absorbed the lessons. His men would be facing even stiffer opposition when their time came.

CHAPTER THREE

THE DEFENDERS

As Allied troops placed inflatable tanks in Kentish fields to fool German air reconnaissance, their counterparts were building plaster horses for much the same reason. The German army of 1944 was, in many ways, little changed from the force it had been in 1918 and was still far from being fully mechanized. Very much a second-class army, the best men were fighting in Russia and the best equipment had been appropriated by the SS, leaving the *Wehrmacht* on the Western Front a relatively under-strength and poorly-equipped fighting force.

Heavy fighting in Russia put pressure on the Germans and the Atlantic Wall defences had become a second priority, especially after the Battle of Kursk when the tide of the war appeared to be turning and the *Ost* battalions of East European volunteers were increasingly viewed with suspicion. These men were sent to France to allow more trustworthy German troops to be used in their place, so that by 1944 the defenders of France were, in many cases, men drawn from dozens of ethnic groups across the occupied territories who could not speak German.[1] Even those units made up of trained Germans were largely filled with men unfit for active service in Russia. When reinforcements arrived on the Cotentin Peninsula, for example, the troops of Colonel Frederick von der Heydte's 6th Parachute Regiment were, on average, half the age of the garrison troops of the 709th Infantry Division already in place.

Command of the German forces along the Atlantic Wall had fallen to Field Marshal Gerd von Rundstedt as Supreme Commander West. Under his command were two army groups: Army Group 'B' took responsibility for the coast from the North Sea to Nantes in southern Brittany, where a line across France from that point to the Swiss border marked the boundary with Army Group 'G'. Command of Army Group 'B' was given to Field Marshal Erwin Rommel early in 1944 and under him, the 7th Army held the defences of Brittany and Normandy as far as the mouth of the River Orne in the east. This waterway marked the boundary with the 15th Army's area of operations which was responsible for covering the coast from that point as far as Holland. Alongside these two armies, General Leo Geyr von Schweppenburg was appointed commander-in-chief of Panzer Group West and controlled the armoured forces across the entire area.

When Rommel inspected the defences of France in 1943, he quickly realized the gulf between Hitler's idea of an Atlantic Wall and the reality of the actual defences then in place. When he assumed tactical command early in 1944, he immediately began a vigorous programme of building and training to make ready for an invasion that he knew was only a matter of time in coming. He firmly believed that any invasion would have to be destroyed on the beaches to prevent an inexorable build-up of matériel which would eventually overwhelm

By 1944, German forces in France had been weakened by the need for the best troops to be deployed in Russia. The defenders of the Atlantic Wall were largely drawn from a mixture of foreign volunteers and wounded or elderly veterans whose role was to delay the Allies until the better-equipped and trained Panzer divisions arrived.

the defences. Even relatively poor-quality troops could achieve this by fighting from strong fortifications with interlocking fields of fire. Nothing in the German experience to date had disproved this. After all, in the blitzkrieg operations of 1940, the much-vaunted Maginot Line had not been breached, it had been bypassed. Rommel wanted to force the Allies into attacking at a point that would stretch their resources, making them even more vulnerable. This would make his planned counterattack more effective if vital equipment had to be unloaded under fire before it could be brought into action. Field Marshal Gerd von Rundstedt, however, favoured the strategy of allowing the Allies to move inland and then launching a rapid counterattack to cut off the supply routes. This, he argued, would remove the heavy naval gunfire support from the ships that would be brought to bear on the coast. Rommel, with his experience in North Africa still fresh in his mind, strongly believed that Allied air power would prevent the movement of reinforcements and that the reaction force needed to be able to respond quickly. Both men argued their cases to Hitler who, following the advice of Germany's 'father' of armoured warfare, General Heinz Guderian, decided to compromise.

Rommel would be given three divisions of armour for immediate defence, and the remainder would be kept further inland. The 21st Panzer Division would be based around Caen, and the others – the 12th SS and the 116th – would be held in reserve between Caen and the Pas-de-Calais ready to be brought forward for von Rundstedt's inland attack should the beaches not be held. Further afield,

A pilot's view of 'Rommel's Asparagus'. These anti-glider poles, often linked by wire and tipped with explosives, were intended to wreak havoc on any attempt to land.

the *Panzer Lehr* were in position near Alençon and the 2nd Panzer Division around Amiens. The significance of the Normandy area was recognized, but the decision was taken that, based on the information coming from agents in Britain, the Pas-de-Calais should be the main focus for planning and construction of the Atlantic Wall. Hitler promised that the remaining tank forces would be released as soon as the enemy's intentions became clear. The difficulty for both commanders was that with only three Panzer divisions readily available between Normandy and Holland, the speed of any counterattack would be slow at best. Worse, Hitler insisted that he should retain control of the tanks. They would not and could not move without his express permission. By now a clumsy German command structure had developed in which the large guns along the Atlantic Wall would remain under naval command until any invading troops actually came ashore, and then and only then would they be given over to the army, while at the same time German armoured forces could only move under the direct orders of the Führer. Any divisional commander would now need to look to Rommel, von Rundstedt and Hitler for orders in a crisis. To complicate matters further, Rommel had no direct control over the Luftwaffe or its units of anti-aircraft artillery or paratroopers and his influence over command and control was fragmented at every level. He did, however, manage to wrest one concession from the convoluted scheme of command and control: the tanks could be moved closer to the coast.[2]

A frantic period of building began as every possible beach landing site was filled with mines, obstacles and, in the fields behind the coast, *Rommelspargel* – 'Rommel's Asparagus' – which were wooden poles sometimes tipped with shells or mines to destroy gliders on landing. By May, Rommel had three infantry divisions on Normandy's Cotentin Peninsula: the 243rd, the 709th and the newly-arrived 91st, along with von der Heydte's paratroopers. Along the Calvados coast he had the 352nd Division facing what would become OMAHA Beach and the 716th stretched along the planned British landing beaches. In effect this meant that, between them, the two under-strength divisions in Calvados had 100km of coastline to defend. Inland, he had his old friends from Africa, the 21st Panzer Division, around Caen under the command of the inexperienced General Edgar Feuchtinger, but with a cadre of highly-skilled officers including Colonel Hans von Luck. The 91st was designated a 'mobile' division, but the Allies would hardly have recognized the German concept of mobility at that stage of the war. At best, it had a couple of trucks to move heavy equipment. Most of its vehicles were horse-drawn, and being 'mobile' often meant that troops had access to bicycles.

The one-legged commander of LXXXIV Corps, General Erich Marcks, knew only too well how weak his men were. Visiting Arromanches, he stared out to sea for a time before turning to his aide. 'If I know the British,' he confided, 'they'll go to church next Sunday for one last time and sail Monday. Army Group B says they're not going to come yet, and that when they do come it'll be at Calais. So I think we'll be welcoming them on Monday, right here.' It was Thursday, 1 June 1944.

In contrast to the static defences scattered along the coastline, the elite 12th SS and 116th Panzer divisions, held in reserve midway between Caen and Calais, were powerful formations. With a nominal strength of 20,540 men, 101 Mk IV tanks and 79 of the latest Panther tanks, the 12th SS based near Evreux was a significant threat. Nearby the 116th, with around 15,000 men, 96 Mk IVs and another 79 Panthers stood ready. Behind them, at Amiens, the 2nd Panzer Division, equally strong, could be ready to move in days. To the south of Caen, at Alençon, the *Panzer Lehr* Division was, in the words of its commander General Fritz Bayerlein, 'the best-equipped panzer division that Germany ever had. It was one hundred per cent armoured; even the infantry were completely armoured.' Guderian had earlier told him: 'With this division alone, you must throw the Allies into the sea. Your objective is the coast – no, not the coast, it is the sea.'[3]

All that stood in the way of the two panzer divisions offering the greatest threat to the entire Normandy invasion were the lightly-armed men of the 6th Airborne.

CHAPTER FOUR

THE PREPARATIONS

The Orne Bridges Mission

Major General Gale had decided that his entire operation hinged on the capture of the Orne bridges. Without the success of the *coup de main* operation to control this link to the beaches, the paras would be trapped. Operation DEADSTICK would be top priority. It was essential that the troops tasked to carry it out arrived on target and on time to maintain the element of surprise. A parachute attack was out of the question as the nearest drop zone would be too far away. Gliders would have to be used.

In February 1944, Squadron Commander Ian Toler of the Glider Pilot Regiment

> *found a message from Wing Headquarters instructing me to provide three of my best crews for a very special operation. I was told they would have to release at 6,000ft and land by moonlight in a small field. As it had to be a surprise attack on an objective that had not yet been disclosed, no landing aids would be possible. I selected six staff sergeants whom I considered from their flying records to be the best pilots.*

In early March 1944 seven glider crews (six for the operation and one as back-up) garnered from the whole of the regiment gathered at Netheravon airfield and were met by their colonel, George Chatterton. Behind him were a number of senior army and Air Force officers. Chatterton pointed out two small triangles marked with broad white tape on the airfield and gave them their briefing:

> *You will be towed at one-minute intervals to 4,000ft, which will take about one hour. You will then release 3 miles away at a point decided by your tug, from where you will be able to see these triangles. Numbers 1, 2 and 3 will land in this one, making a right-hand circuit, and 4, 5 and 6 on t'other from a left-hand circuit. Now hop off for lunch. All gliders are ready and assembled on the towpath. Take off 1300 hrs.*

To Chatterton's evident relief, all six landed exactly on target, but some senior RAF officers were still doubtful so the exercise was repeated the following day. Again, the gliders landed exactly on target – surprising themselves as much as the RAF – and Operation DEADSTICK was under way. The fourteen glider pilots were kept sequestered in one Nissen hut at Tarrant Rushton airfield with a lieutenant placed in charge. They had their own transport and their own independent operation directed by two RAF pilots: Flight Lieutenants Tom Grant and Keith Miller, both tug/glider specialists who provided the briefings, courses, winds and timings on every flight.

Glider pilot Jim Wallwork remembers that training for Operation DEADSTICK was 'all a bit half-arsed at first. A daylight tow was made at various times, apparently when Tarrant Rushton airfield was not too busy, which as two operational squadrons were based there was not very often.' Flying by timings onto the field in daylight proved no problem. Soon, though, the crews were facing more of a challenge, flying with heavily-shaded goggles to simulate night-time conditions into ever-smaller LZs. By June, they had flown forty-two practice missions and were confident of success.

As the pilots practised, Gale briefed Brigadier Nigel Poett on the operation. Poett, in charge of the division's paratroops, would be responsible for reinforcing the *coup de main* party as soon as possible after landing and would therefore be given command of the operation. The troops, though, would come from Brigadier Hugh Kindersley's Airlanding Brigade. Gale approached him and asked his opinion of his company commanders. One name stood out. Major John Howard, a former Oxford policeman, had demonstrated time and again his skill and leadership. A three-day exercise was laid on.

AWARD CITATION

MAJOR JOHN HOWARD, 2ND BATTALION OXFORDSHIRE AND BUCKINGHAMSHIRE LIGHT INFANTRY

DISTINGUISHED SERVICE ORDER

Major Howard was in comd of the airborne force which landed by glider and secured the bridges over the R. ORNE and CAEN Canal near BENOUVILLE by coup de main on 6-6-44. Throughout the planning and execution of the operation Major Howard displayed the greatest leadership, judgement, courage and coolness. His personal example and the enthusiasm which he put behind his task carried all his subordinates with him, and the operation proved a complete success.

Howard's D Company of 2/OBLI, riding in lorries to simulate gliders, was tasked with seizing three small bridges from a defending force of paras and holding them until relieved. They achieved their goal after what Howard described as 'a first-class fight' and were singled out for praise by Gale, Kindersley and Poett. A short time later Howard was summoned to the office of the Ox & Bucks Commanding Officer, Lieutenant Colonel Roberts, and told of his mission. He was to enlarge his own company with two platoons and offered his pick of the battalion. He chose two platoons of B Company under Lieutenants Sandy Smith and Dennis Fox.

Howard considered how he was supposed to capture the bridges if all it took was for a single German to press a button and detonate the demolition charges. In his 1948 account *The 6th Airborne Division in Normandy*, Gale wrote that

> *there is always or nearly always a slip between the cup and the lip; orders are vague; there is uncertainty; has the moment arrived or should*

> *one wait? Who is the individual responsible both for working the switch and for ordering the bridges to be blown? These questions are age-old and on the doubts that might exist in some German mind or minds at the critical moment I based the plan. But a moment or two was all that I knew we would get. The assault on the bridges must, therefore, come like a bolt from the blue.*

The two bridges were vital and planners knew that both would be prepared for demolition. Detailed models were made based on the available information (the best coming from a pre-war picture postcard donated by a member of the public in response to an appeal for information on Europe) and from these, the likely placing of demolition charges was worked out. The task of removing the charges fell to 2 Platoon, 249 Field Company Royal Engineers (Airborne) under Captain Jock Neilson and Lieutenant Jack Bence, whose men now joined Howard's command. Initially the sappers, like all paras, resented being relegated to the role of glider-borne troops, but the two units soon began to work together, recognizing the importance of their task. Once the bridges were secure, Bence would be responsible for assessing them for their load class: the weight of vehicle the bridges could carry and whether they would be able to support the Sherman tanks making their way from the beaches to link with the airborne force. This involved taking measurements with a tape measure and a footrule and then applying mathematical formulae, all of which would need to be completed under fire.

The sappers were distributed throughout the *coup de main* force with one officer or NCO and four sappers in each of the six gliders. Each glider party was fully briefed to act independently and to search the same places for demolition charges on their allotted target and on the other bridge in case only one group arrived. To cover all eventualities, their equipment included scaling ladders, hand-axes, small crowbars, torches and pliers as well as a folding canvas assault boat and an inflatable dinghy. The last two items were part of an emergency plan in case the bridges were blown, but there was another hazard to consider. The water level in the canal was controlled by locks at Ouistreham. If these were destroyed by the enemy, the canal waterway at Bénouville would be reduced to a few feet in width with steep muddy slopes on either side.

The contingency plan was for the 7th Parachute Battalion (7 Para), dropping north of Ranville, to secure a bridgehead to the west of Bénouville and the canal which would involve ferrying the troops across the water gaps. A small detachment of four sappers under the command of a Royal Engineers sergeant would drop with 7 Para along with thirty inflatable RAF-issue dinghies and 500 fathoms of rope carried during the drop by 7 Para troops in their kitbags. Two hours after the first drop, the remainder of 2 Platoon's engineers would land in four gliders carrying lightweight rafts capable of taking the 6-pounder anti-tank gun. More RAF dinghies and rope made up the rest of the load together with two 30ft rolls of 'chespaling' (a temporary road surface laid on hessian sacking sprayed with oil paint), which would be rolled over the muddy banks. In the event that the *coup de main* was a success, this equipment would be stockpiled on the east bank of the River Orne in case a counterattack was launched to destroy the bridges after capture.[1]

In training, Howard got everything he asked for. Bridges near Exeter that were a close match to the target were found. In exercises, the defenders of the

D Company, 2/Ox and Bucks Light Infantry. (Courtesy of Denis Edwards)

bridges wore German uniforms, carried German weapons and spoke in German to each other. Any equipment he wanted was given top priority. When the 21st Panzer Division moved into the Caen area on 23 May, Howard knew about it the next day. When German paratroopers were seen in the area, he was told immediately. He began pushing his men hard. In addition to their glider drills, they learned to handle boats in case the bridges were blown. The only thing in short supply was food so, during the boat exercises, the men indulged in a little fishing using grenades. Morale was high as training reached its end and a wild night out in Exeter resulted in the entire local police force being called out to round up the company and escort it back to camp. In late May they moved to Tarrant Rushton, their final stop on the way to France.[2]

It was here that they met the glider pilots for the first time and were briefed about their mission. Jim Wallwork and the other pilots were quickly absorbed into the unit, but spent hours locked away in a hut where reconnaissance photographs of the targets had been strung together to create a flight simulator. Over and over the pilots flew the route to their target. 'It was absolutely fantastic,' Wallwork said, declaring the exercise 'invaluable'. Then, on 30 May, new reconnaissance shots arrived. Holes had appeared all around the landing zone, ready for anti-glider poles to be installed. Howard's fear that word had leaked was soon dispelled as similar holes were appearing all along the coast. Approaching Wallwork, Howard asked what he thought their chances were. Grinning, Wallwork told him that the poles were a benefit since 'those poles will take something off one wing and something off the other wing – it's just damned cheap plywood, you know – and those poles will pull us up absolutely beautifully.'

One thing remained. Around the bridge approaches were coils of barbed wire. Could Wallwork use the nose of the glider to break through? Wallwork explained that he could try, but that the gliders were overloaded and would be difficult to land anywhere, let alone with any precision. They would need to lose weight. Reluctantly, Howard agreed to drop men from the mission. He then had to explain to several heartbroken men why they were being left behind. Finally, the force was declared ready to go.

The Merville Battery Mission

On 2 April, Lieutenant Colonel Terence Otway, a former Royal Ulster Rifles officer now commanding 9 Para, received orders to prepare for a special task: silencing the seemingly impregnable battery of guns at Merville, overlooking SWORD Beach across which the British 3rd Division would land on D-Day.[3] Aerial reconnaissance in May 1944 reported four deeply entrenched casemates, each capable of holding a 150mm gun. Such weapons had a range of 14,600 yards (8.3 miles) and could fire a 96lb shell every 15 to 20 seconds. Sited only about 3 miles from one of the main British landing sites, the battery was therefore a very real threat. It was deemed so important a target that air attacks would also be attempted and if, by 0500 hrs on the morning of the landings, Otway had not signalled the fleet, naval gunfire would be directed at the battery whether his men were still in the vicinity or not.

AWARD CITATION

LIEUTENANT COLONEL TERENCE OTWAY, 9TH PARACHUTE BATTALION

DISTINGUISHED SERVICE ORDER

For conspicuous bravery and outstanding leadership. This officer led 150 men of his bn on the successful attack of the Sallenelles battery. He personally directed the attack and organised the successful cleaning up of the enemy strongpoints under heavy enemy mortar and machine-gun fire. He led the attack on and successfully held Le Plein until relieved by another formation. On arrival in the Le Mesnil area he succeeded in beating off two major enemy attacks of several hours duration by his magnificent leadership of his numerically very weak and tired bn. His utter disregard of personal danger has been an inspiration for all his men.

The site itself consisted of four gun emplacements set in an arc, each protected by more than 6ft of steel-reinforced concrete camouflaged and protected by earth banks. A 400-yard anti-tank ditch, 15ft wide and 10ft deep, ran along the northern perimeter and around the site ran two belts of barbed wire between 90 and 170 yards apart. The inner belt was 10ft wide and up to 8ft high with a minefield between it and the outer wire. It was thought that around 160 to 200 men garrisoned the battery and the site was ringed with five camouflaged machine-gun emplacements and a further fifteen weapons pits, each with four or five machine guns along with three 20mm anti-aircraft weapon positions, each capable of being used in a ground defence role. The Merville battery was a formidable target to say the least.

Otway also learned that the commanding officer of the battery was newly-installed in his post. His predecessor had been fond of a drink and was well-known around the area for his excesses. When Merville held its local fair, the drunken colonel took a ride on a fast merry-go-round and local inhabitants bribed the operator of the ride to keep it going as fast and as long as possible. The colonel lasted two hours before the ride ended and was last seen being carried away by an orderly.[4] Whatever benefits a drunken commander may have provided for Otway's force, they had now evaporated. Now, with only two months to prepare, Otway, like Howard, was given free rein to train his men and get them ready.

A location was found at West Woodhay near Newbury in Berkshire where the terrain was very similar to that of Normandy. The spot, however, was prime agricultural land and objections were sure to be raised. Otway needed to obtain the relevant permissions from no fewer than seven different Whitehall ministries and had to do a lot of smooth talking to local inhabitants, some of whom 'had to be pacified by drinks in the mess' to secure the land, but so vital was the mission that after just forty-eight hours, it was his. Within a week, a team of

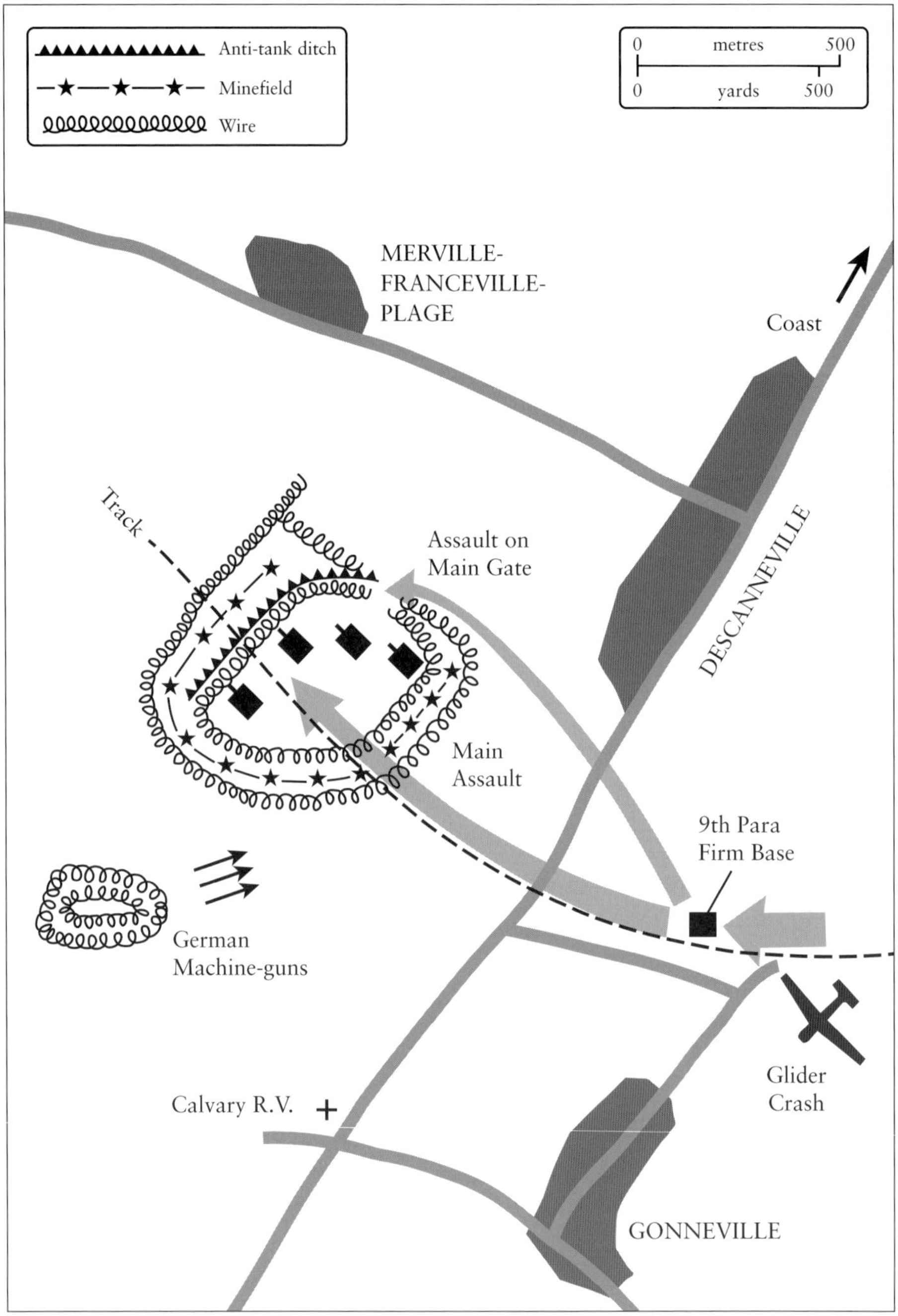

The Merville Battery assault.

sappers using four earth excavators and six large bulldozers brought on tank transporters from as far away as Liverpool and Plymouth had worked around the clock – 'the hours of darkness being illuminated by the headlights of vehicles' – to create a full-sized replica battery.

The plan of assault was complex. An advance party would drop at 0020 hrs along with the pathfinders of the 22nd Independent Parachute Company and the 1st Battalion of the Canadian Parachute Regiment (1 Cdn Para). The three companies of Canadians were tasked to secure the areas around the DZ and to eliminate selected targets nearby. One group from 'A' Company would provide security for the left flank of 9 Para before taking up their own positions around the crossroads in the nearby village of Le Mesnil.

As the advance party of 9 Para moved towards Merville, a force of 100 RAF Lancaster and Halifax bombers was to attack the battery at 0030 hrs with 4,000lb bombs. A lucky strike might mean that the paras would not be required, but planners knew that this was unlikely. The air attack would serve to soften up the target and to create cover around the site for the men on the ground.

The advance party would split into small groups that went under the collective name of 'Trowbridge', named after a British naval captain sent by Lord Nelson to recce the French fleet before the Battle of Trafalgar in 1805. The task of the first 'Trowbridge' party, made up of Major George Smith, his batman and two NCOs, was to infiltrate the defences of the battery by cutting through the wire, clearing a path through the minefield and assessing the bomb damage. The second 'Trowbridge' group was to investigate a nearby target, suspected of being a decoy. Meanwhile Major Allan Parry would lead a third party to locate the rendezvous (RV) and set up a signalling lamp to guide in 9 Para after the drop. They were also equipped with 'Ducks, Bakelite' – whistle calls like those used by hunters and the British equivalent of the famous 'Crickets' used by US paratroops – to help in indicating their position to stragglers.

The main body would then drop at 0050 hrs, bringing with them five gliders carrying heavy weapons and a team of Royal Engineers with mine-clearance equipment. Once on the ground, everyone was expected to reach the RV by 0235 hrs and be in position to attack by 0400 hrs. The breaching party, led by Lieutenant the Honourable Paul Greenway and engineer Captain Tony Jackson would then begin to place Bangalore torpedoes under the wire and to clear a path through the minefields. A diversionary attack at the main entrance by German-speaking paras would take place at 0430 hrs to coincide with the arrival of the *coup de main* force in three gliders. Armed with Sten submachine guns and flame-throwers, this force would immediately attack the casemates directly from their landing site inside the perimeter. They would be joined by the main assault force equipped with medium machine guns and an anti-tank troop who would use their weapons against the heavy steel doors of the bunkers after they had cut their way through the wire as the attack started. Also among the assault group would be a team of forward observers whose job would be to call in naval gunfire from HMS *Arethusa* if the battery could not be taken in time. If that all went well, 9 Para would then move to a second RV and assault the naval radar station and HQ at Sallenelles before finally taking up position around Amfreville.

Without explaining the task ahead, Otway gathered the men of his 'A' Company in the mess hall and called for volunteers for a dangerous mission by glider. Every man stepped forward. Gradually, the force was whittled down by selecting as many unmarried men as possible, causing rumours of a 'suicide job' to circulate. Fred Millward was relieved not to be selected:

> *I didn't want to go in the gliders. I'd flown in one before. I had a trip in a Horsa and oh, the smell of the vomit! It was the actual movement of the thing, because not only did you go up and down, you also had the tugging. It wasn't a very nice feeling.*

In the plan for the attack on the battery, the selected men, under Captain Gordon-Brown – unsurprisingly earning the tag of 'G-B Force' – would be required to land on top of the casemates and attack with flame-throwers and small arms as the remainder of the battalion stormed the outer defences. Lieutenant Hugh Pond, one of those selected, was with the group when it was

> *taken to a small aerodrome and [we] made our first acquaintance with the glider and the glider pilots. We were horrified at the three-ply wooden structure and considered it more a joke, a toy, than a vehicle for going to war in.... We climbed into the 'matchbox' and belted up. There were twenty-eight of us in all and we had a good laugh when we were introduced to the funnel which was the urinal. It doesn't take much to make a bunch of nervous parachutists laugh!*

The flight went well and the G-B Force began to think their 'hazardous operation' might not be so bad after all.

For weeks the pilots flew repeat practice landings into a circle painted on the airfield and joined the paras in street-fighting exercises in bomb-damaged areas of London. Pilot Bill Shannon was suffering from a bout of 'flu at the time and passed out during one such exercise. He woke to find everyone had returned to barracks, leaving him to walk home. 'It wasn't so much the walk,' he remembered, 'it was the fact that I was wearing German uniform and carrying a Schmeisser. Not one person challenged me, the whole way. In fact I lost count of the number of times I was saluted!'[5] The exercises continued on the full-scale model of the battery but, as Hugh Pond recalled,

> *when it came to live ammunition exercises we were told that we couldn't wreck a glider just for practice so we were marched into the centre of the mock-up battery and stood there, feeling rather silly, waiting for our comrades to arrive and, as one bright spark put it, waiting to be shot by our own people!*

To avoid that risk, passwords were hurriedly arranged. Captain Gordon-Brown, an architect in civilian life, came up with the idea of painting a luminous skull and crossbones on the breast of their jump smocks. Improvising with toothbrushes and shaving brushes, G-B Force happily joined in the bravado until someone pointed out what a great aiming-point the brightly luminous insignia made.

* * *

Meanwhile, the rest of the division was also engaged in intensive training. On 4 April, the GPR's 'D' Squadron supplied thirty Horsas for Exercise Dreme, a mass landing on Salisbury Plain, but on the day the LZ was covered by low cloud. Twenty-two gliders crashed and were written off during the landings. Worse, a Stirling tug and Horsa combination elected to fly below the cloud and slammed into a low hill at 140 mph. The six-man crew of the tug, the glider pilots and their twenty-six passengers were

An abandoned Horsa.

all killed. Bill Musitano, another pilot on the exercise, wrote afterwards that 'it was said that the largest human remains were in their boots.' It was a sobering portent of what was to come.

Slowly, the division was made ready. In 3 Para Brigade, Brigadier James Hill stressed the importance of four objectives: speed, control, simplicity and fire effect. His paratroopers would not be able to carry much equipment with them, but this would give them the advantage of speed of movement. 'If you could give orders twice as fast as anyone else you could gain ten minutes on the enemy,' he claimed. Having control over easily-recognized goals with clear instructions would use this speed to its best effect. Finally, since the lightly-armed paras would not be able to carry extra ammunition on the already overloaded flights, every shot had to count and fire effect was stressed at every level. Hill knew that the brigade would have to fight at night so for one week every month it was sent out to operate at night, and the entire brigade munched on carrots in an attempt to improve their night vision. Stories had circulated that 'Cat's Eyes' Cunningham, a fighter pilot who achieved a number of night-time kills had attributed his success to eating carrots. It was only many years later that Hill discovered that the story had been put out to cover the use of radar.

As the operation approached, the men were pushed harder and harder. Even the clerks and telephone operators of Hill's HQ took part in gruelling two-hour marches carrying 60lb packs. To encourage his men to enjoy church parade, Hill even insisted that they carry their packs to church, stacking them under guard outside. After the service, they would be taken on 20-mile route marches and it was after one of these that the local Women's Institute sent a group to complain about Hill's 'encouragement' of his men as they passed through Bulford. Hill also introduced a team of parachuting German Shepherd dogs to act as messengers. Using parachutes designed for dropping bicycles, the teams soon found that some of the dogs became enthusiastic paratroopers, needing to be held back once the aircraft door opened. The rationale was that the dogs would act as runners, but Hill admitted later that their primary purpose was to keep up his men's morale.

THE HORSA GLIDER

AIRSPEED AS51 HORSA Mk I and Mk II
Wingspan: 88ft
Length: 68ft
Height: 20.3ft
Crew: Pilot and co-pilot
Weight total: 15,750lb; cargo: 7,380lb
Loadings: 28 troops, two jeeps or one jeep and one 6-pounder gun (or equivalent).
Tow speed: 160 mph
Glide ratio: 7.2
Towplanes: Albemarle, Wellington, Dakota, Lancaster, Stirling, Halifax.

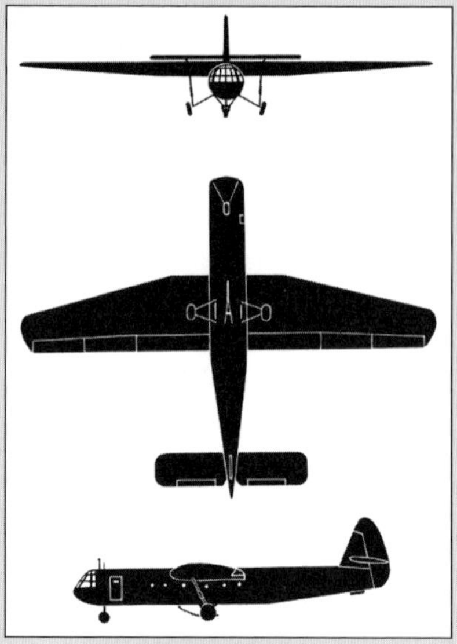

Horsa glider silhouette.

First flown on 27 March 1942, the Hamilcar was the largest wooden aircraft built during the war, prompting the US army's glider procurement officer to call it 'the biggest hunk of airplane I have ever seen put together.' It featured a nose-opening door that opened automatically and could carry the Tetrarch or M22 Locust light tanks. These tanks started their engines during the approach and could be in action just fifteen seconds after landing, although there were incidents in which they started forward while still in flight and caused fatal crashes. A total of 412 aircraft were produced.

In response to the German attack on the Belgian fortress of Ében-Émael in May 1940, Churchill issued an order for Britain to create an airborne force of paratroopers and glider-borne units. To meet the need for a troop-carrying aircraft, the Horsa, built mainly by former furniture manufacturers so as not to affect the production of combat aircraft, first flew on 12 September 1941, just ten months after the specifications had been issued.

The plywood construction of the Horsa soon earned it the nickname of 'the matchbox' by the RAF crews who towed it. Among the Americans who flew a number of Horsas into Normandy, it had another nickname: 'the flying morgue'. When the makers of the film account of the D-Day landings *The Longest Day* had replicas built, the Air Ministry refused permission for them to be flown across the Channel. It was, they said, 'an inherently dangerous design'.

Even as production reached its peak at the end of the war, the glider's replacement was entering service as army pilots began their conversion to helicopters in 1945. A total of 3,655 Horsas were built during the war and the aircraft remained in service for re-supply operations in the Middle East. The Glider Pilot Regiment was formally disbanded in 1957 to re-emerge as today's Army Air Corps.

The original plan had called for the glider reinforcements to be flown into the open ground north of Ranville as early as possible on the morning of D-Day, but the appearance of the anti-glider poles that had caused Howard such concern had been noted across the whole landing area. Lieutenant Colonel Frank Lowman, Commander Royal Engineers, was shown the air photographs just minutes before being summoned to Gale's office. 'Have you seen these air photos, Frank?' asked the general. 'Do you realise what they mean and what do you propose to do about them?' Lowman was ready: 'Yes, Sir. They are anti-airlanding poles and we shall have to blow them down and carry them away.'

Plans for reinforcement by glider were put back to allow time for sappers of 591 (Antrim) Parachute Squadron of the Royal Engineers to clear lanes through the poles for the aircraft of Operations TONGA and later MALLARD to land. Close study of the air photographs showed that the obstructions were mainly wooden poles 12 to 18in in diameter, reinforced in places with metal girders all standing around 15ft high and sunk into holes about 4ft deep. They were spaced between 30 and 60 yards apart, but linked by wires and sometimes tipped with mines or shells. The preparations were far from completed and many areas simply had the holes ready for the poles to be delivered, but those already in place were a real threat.

Lowton and Chatterton decided that for the initial glider force of seventy Horsa gliders carrying Divisional HQ and one 6-pounder Anti-Tank Battery and due to land during the night, two strips, each 1,000 x 60 yards, would need to be cleared so that each strip would then be able to take thirty-five gliders. Later the main force of around 140 gliders, including the much larger Hamilcars carrying tanks and 17-pounder Anti-Tank Batteries would be due to land at 2100 hrs on the evening of D-Day and two strips further to the east would have to be cleared. The size of the Hamilcars meant that these new strips would need to be 90 yards wide. Each strip would also need an approach area cleared where the poles would be dropped, but did not need to be moved out of the way. It was a lot of work without heavy engineering equipment and a technique needed to be worked out for it.

The sheer size of the aircraft is obvious in this picture in which 200 men of the Glider Pilot Regiment and their RAF colleagues gather in front of one of the squadron's Hamilcar gliders. (Courtesy of GPRA)

Stan Jeavons, 13 Para, whose unorthodox approach to using military transport almost led to him missing D-Day.

Permission was granted for 100 trees to be felled in the New Forest and used to create a replica of the obstacles on an area of Salisbury Plain so that 591 Squadron could set to work. Each pole, it was decided, would be dealt with in the same way. First, an area 6in deep x 12in wide would be dug around its base. Next, a 5lb charge of plastic explosive, packed into a bicycle inner tube and carried by the engineers as bandoliers during the drop would be wrapped around the pole and used to blast through. As each pole dropped, it would be manhandled to the side of the strip and laid at a 45-degree angle to allow the gliders to turn off. Then the hole would be backfilled and stamped down. Each strip would need six teams of infantrymen to act as porters under the guidance of an engineer NCO and practice runs showed that the night strips could be made ready in just ninety minutes. The longer day strips would take two hours. A total of 4 officers, 12 NCOs and 120 men from the 13th Parachute Battalion (13 Para) would provide the labour, with cover provided by the 12th Parachute Battalion (12 Para). With the gliders scheduled to arrive at 0320 hrs, two engineer reconnaissance teams would drop at 0030 hrs to tape out the two strips, followed at 0100 hrs by the main party, allowing them time to regroup before setting to work.

Across the division, specialist teams rehearsed their role in the coming invasion. Not everyone, though, used their training in the way in which it was intended. Lieutenant Stan Jeavons of 13 Para was on exercise in Scotland when news came through that his wife had given birth to a son, Roger. Jeavons applied for leave and was refused. As the unit flew back to its base in southern England, Jeavons, knowing that he may never have another chance to see his child, waited until the Dakota was over the Birmingham area and then calmly opened the door and jumped. A few hours later, when he reached his home, he found two military policemen waiting for him. A neighbour, Fred Blades, remembered what happened next: 'Stan told the M.P.s they could do it the hard way and he was fingering his Sten gun, or they could let him inside the house to hold his baby and then he'd go quietly. That's what happened.' He was given just five minutes and then escorted back to his unit. He then jumped again, this time with permission, with the battalion on D-Day.[6]

Finally, in late May, the division filtered into its transit camps; the last stop before France. The gates were locked and the long wait began.

CHAPTER FIVE

READY TO GO

Eventually, the men of the 6th Airborne were assembled and told that the invasion was to take place on 5 June and that the target area was Normandy. Then the briefings began. Over the coming days, the men would pore over maps, aerial photographs and sand table models of the intended DZs to familiarize themselves with the target and were assigned their individual tasks. Captain Huw Wheldon of the 1st Royal Ulster Rifles later recalled that

> *it was an extraordinary period. Maps and models were produced and studied. To the question 'How could you get unobserved from the inn to the Mayor's house in such and such a town?' troops could answer 'You get into the garden behind the inn, move down the stream as far as the old broken-down car and then go up through the hole in the wall and through the orchard, and there you are.' Everybody learnt exactly what his job would be. It was like working for an examination.*[1]

A glider pilot and his RAF towplane pilot at a briefing prior to the mission. Despite initial difficulties, the two services worked well together.

As the time approached, ammunition and equipment were distributed and in each unit, men settled down to write letters home, knowing that they would not be posted until after it had been confirmed that they had landed in France. By then, some of the authors would already be dead. At Broadwell, 9 Para's chaplain, the Reverend J. Gwinnett, conducted a drumhead service to dedicate a special Pegasus flag made for them by the Women's Voluntary Services at Oxford and donated by the men of the Permanent Staff of the Transit Camp who, as a result of parachute operations, were no longer fit for action and would not be going with them. Years later, many of those present could still remember Gwinnett's theme: 'Fear knocked at the door, Faith opened it and there was nothing there.' Then the men were told that bad weather had put the whole operation back by twenty-four hours. Although the weather over the British airfields was not bad, a storm was blowing out in the Channel. Forecasters spoke of the weather for the 5th 'clearing temporarily after a doubtful start', while across the Channel the German meteorological office confidently predicted that no invasion could take place that night or the next, but Allied planners had other ideas. If the invasion did not go ahead soon, it would be another two weeks before tide conditions would again be suitable and by then the element of surprise would be gone. At sea, the naval armada kept circling, waiting for orders. If they did not receive the signal to go soon, they would run out of fuel.

That evening Eisenhower met with his senior advisors as wind and rain rattled the windows of his HQ at Southwick House. Group Captain J.M. Stagg, the senior meteorological officer at Supreme Headquarters, Allied Expeditionary Force (SHAEF), had already delivered the gloomy prediction that had postponed the invasion. Now, at 2130 hrs, he arrived with the latest report, forecasting a break in the storm. General Kenneth Strong described how 'a cheer went up. You never heard middle-aged men cheer like that!' The rain, Stagg said, would stop before daybreak and it would be followed by thirty-six hours of 'more or less clear weather'. Air Vice Marshal Leigh-Mallory, the senior air commander, lost his enthusiasm at the news. 'More or less' clear weather gave no guarantee that the airborne element could be landed in the right place or that air support could be effective. His deputy, Air Marshal Arthur Tedder, agreed. Eisenhower's chief of staff, Walter Smith, thought it 'a helluva gamble but it's the best possible gamble.' Eisenhower then turned to General Bernard Montgomery and asked if he saw any reason to delay. Montgomery said simply, 'I would say – Go!' SHAEF's high command was split. Eisenhower knew that he must make the final decision. He paced the room for several minutes and then, fifteen minutes after Stagg had delivered his report, Eisenhower declared, 'I am quite positive that the order must be given.'

Five hours later, Eisenhower returned to Southwick House to find Stagg looking pleased. The weather, he said, was improving and he could be certain that it would also improve for the next twenty-four hours, but would then close in again. The first waves could land but the follow-up may be disrupted. Again, Eisenhower consulted his advisors. Montgomery and Smith still wanted to go. Admiral Ramsay, in charge of naval support, was concerned about his ability to provide naval gunfire support, but agreed the risk was worth taking. Only the airmen still thought the risk too great. With ships reaching the point of no return, Eisenhower began pacing again. After a while, he turned to his commanders and said quietly, 'OK, let's go.' Later that day, he sat at his desk to write a press release. It began:

> *Our landings...have failed and I have withdrawn the troops. My decision to attack at this time and place was based upon the best information available. The troops, the air and the Navy did all that bravery and devotion to duty could do. If any blame or fault attaches to the attempt it is mine alone.*[2]
>
> *'Despite the weather being far from perfect,' recalled Sergeant Clem Keeble of the 8th Parachute Battalion (8 Para), 'we were told the next day that we were going that evening, so after breakfast on the 5th we went across to the airfield, drew our parachutes, made our way to our various aircraft and after placing our 'chutes on the seats, we had a chat with the aircrew and then made our way back to camp. Later in the morning there was an open-air church service, followed by a hot meal and we were then told to rest because it would be some while before we got another chance, but I don't think that many were able to take advantage, we were too keyed up.'*

At the airfields, the delay meant that tension was building to breaking-point. As nervous men cleaned and re-cleaned their weapons, accidents began to happen. Among the men of 9 Para, Lance Corporal Edward Hull of A Company, one of those scheduled to land with Hugh Pond's glider force inside the battery, was hit by a rifle bullet as he carried new orders to Company HQ. His platoon commander and the padre obtained special permission to leave camp to visit him at the 107th General Hospital in Oxford where they found the 25-year-old in tears at the thought of missing the operation. He died the next day.

Hamilcar gliders line up ready for Operation MALLARD, the resupply flights on the evening of 6 June.

With the division sealed in its marshalling camps, the only link to the outside world came through the postal unit who made the final delivery of mail on the morning of 5 June. After that, all private outgoing mail was collected by the postal unit and sent to holding offices where it was held until after the news of the landings had been made public knowledge by the news agencies before it could be released into the postal system.

For Clem Keeble, the operation began at about 1900 hrs on the 5th when he and his men gathered their kit. It was a slow process, considering what each man carried. Lieutenant Colonel A.R. Clark of 13 Para later remembered the contents of the kitbag he carried: a change of underwear and socks, washing and shaving kit, gym shoes, gas cape and groundsheet, full water bottle, respirator, mess tin with his knife, fork and spoon, drinking mug and a forty-eight-hour ration pack. Added to this were 2lb of plastic explosive, two belts of .303 Vickers MG ammunition, two filled Bren magazines, a shovel, a pair of wire-cutters and three of the heavy and cumbersome spare radio batteries. These, of course, may not be readily to hand when he landed, so Clark carried what he considered the most important items in his webbing and jacket pockets: his Sten gun and spare magazines, two hand grenades, a holster with a .45 automatic and spare ammunition and 2lb of plastic explosive in his pocket along with a Webley revolver and ammunition. Tucked away inside his Denison smock was a hunting horn to signal his men, a spare pullover, a knitted hat and red beret as well as an escape kit containing a compass, currency and maps. More maps and a message pad were fitted into his trouser pocket, as were a first-aid kit, field dressing and morphine syringe. A Commando fighting knife went into a hidden pocket in the seam of his trousers. A thick section of toggle rope completed the list. Other men carried more.[3]

Across the airfields of southern England, the men once more made their way across to the waiting aircraft and sat on the grass with a sandwich and a mug of tea as they waited for the final order to 'fit chutes and emplane'. One soldier quietly scooped up a handful of soil and poured it into an envelope and gently put the package into his pocket, saying 'God knows when we shall see England again.'[4]

Once the heavily-laden paras had helped each other get on board, the planes' engines roared into life and they began to taxi round the airfield perimeters until, one by one, they lumbered into the air. For hours, the aircraft circled the country in an ever-increasing flock as they waited for the signal to go:

> *'Below us in Southampton Water,' one veteran wrote in 1946, 'lay assembled the greatest armada of all time. How reassuring it was to think that soon they too would be over the other side with our supplies. As we looked down it seemed hard to believe that there was any water between the Isle of Wight and the mainland, for the ships made Southampton Water look like a gigantic dry-dock.'*

At their base, Major Howard watched as his men headed towards their gliders. 'It was an amazing sight,' he wrote. 'The smaller chaps were visibly sagging at the knees under the amount of kit they had to carry.' Just before they boarded, he tried to give them a pep talk, but found that he was 'a sentimental man at heart, for which reason I don't think I am a good soldier. I found offering my thanks to these chaps a devil of a job. My voice just wasn't my own.' At 22.56 hrs, the first aircraft of the *coup de main* force began to roll down the runway.

CHAPTER SIX

PEGASUS BRIDGE

At 0007 hrs on Tuesday, 6 June 1944, tug pilot Wing Commander Duder wished the crew of the glider he was towing good luck and released the cable at 6,000ft over the French coast. At that moment five other gliders also cast off into free flight southwards for just over three minutes, made a 90-degree turn onto their second course for another two and a half minutes followed by another 90-degree turn which brought them directly over their target. In the cockpit of PF800, a Horsa glider with the chalk number 91, co-pilot John Ainsworth peered at his stopwatch, counting down the seconds: 'Five... four... three... two... one.... Bingo, right turn to starboard onto course.' Pilot Jim Wallwork looked around and could see the moonlight glinting off the surface of the river and canal below him.

> *'So then,' he recalls, 'to hell with the course. I knew my height; I knew how far away I was, so it was a case of by guess and by God from then on. I didn't complete the crosswind leg, so I bowled down and landed rather quickly. There was a feeling of the land rushing up and I landed probably at about ninety-five instead of at eighty-five, and 10 miles per hour in the dark looks like a lot.'*

As the glider hit the ground, Wallwork shouted 'Stream' and Ainsworth released the arrester parachute which lifted the tail, forcing the nose into the ground. Immediately the impact tore off the wheels and bounced the glider back into the air, but the parachute did its job and they hit the ground again, this time on the skids. Wallwork shouted 'Jettison' and Ainsworth pressed the button to release the parachute. The glider had slowed, but was careering along the ground at 60 mph in a shower of sparks that made its passengers think they were already under fire.

> *'There was the usual slight bump,' recalls Eddie Edwards, one of those aboard, 'a small jerk and a much heavier thump as the glider made contact with the ground, but only for a moment. It jerked again, shuddered, left the ground for a second or two, bumped over the rough surface and lurched forward like a bucking bronco. We sped forward, bouncing up and down on our hard wooden seats as the vehicle lost contact with the ground, then came down again with another heavy thump, a tug and a jerk. For a few moments it appeared that we were in for a comparatively smooth landing, but just as that thought flashed through my mind the darkness filled with a stream of brilliant sparks as the glider lost its wheels and the skid hit some stony ground. There followed a sound like a giant canvas sheet being viciously ripped apart, then a mighty crash like a clap of thunder and my body seemed to be moving in several directions at*

once. Moments later the crippled glider skidded and bounced over the uneven ground to slide finally to a juddering halt, whereupon I found myself perched in a very strange position at an uneven angle. I peered into a misty blue and greyish haze. From somewhere out in endless space there zoomed towards me a long tracer-like stream of multicoloured lights, like a host of shooting stars that moved towards me at high speed. I realized after a moment that I was not being shot at. I was simply concussed and

Pegasus Bridge, with Gliders 1, 2 and 3, all within yards of their target. (Courtesy of GPRA)

seeing stars! The noise from the landing had ceased very suddenly and was replaced by an ominous silence. No-one stirred, nothing moved. My immediate thought was "God help me – we must all be dead".... The exit door had been right beside my seat. Now there was only a mass of twisted wood and fabric across the doorway and we had to use the butts of our rifles to smash our way out.'

It was 0016 hrs. D-Day had begun.[1]

Before setting out, Wallwork and Ainsworth had studied the reconnaissance pictures carefully. They had promised to try to breach the wire around the bridge, but knew that this would mean hitting the embankment. At best, they

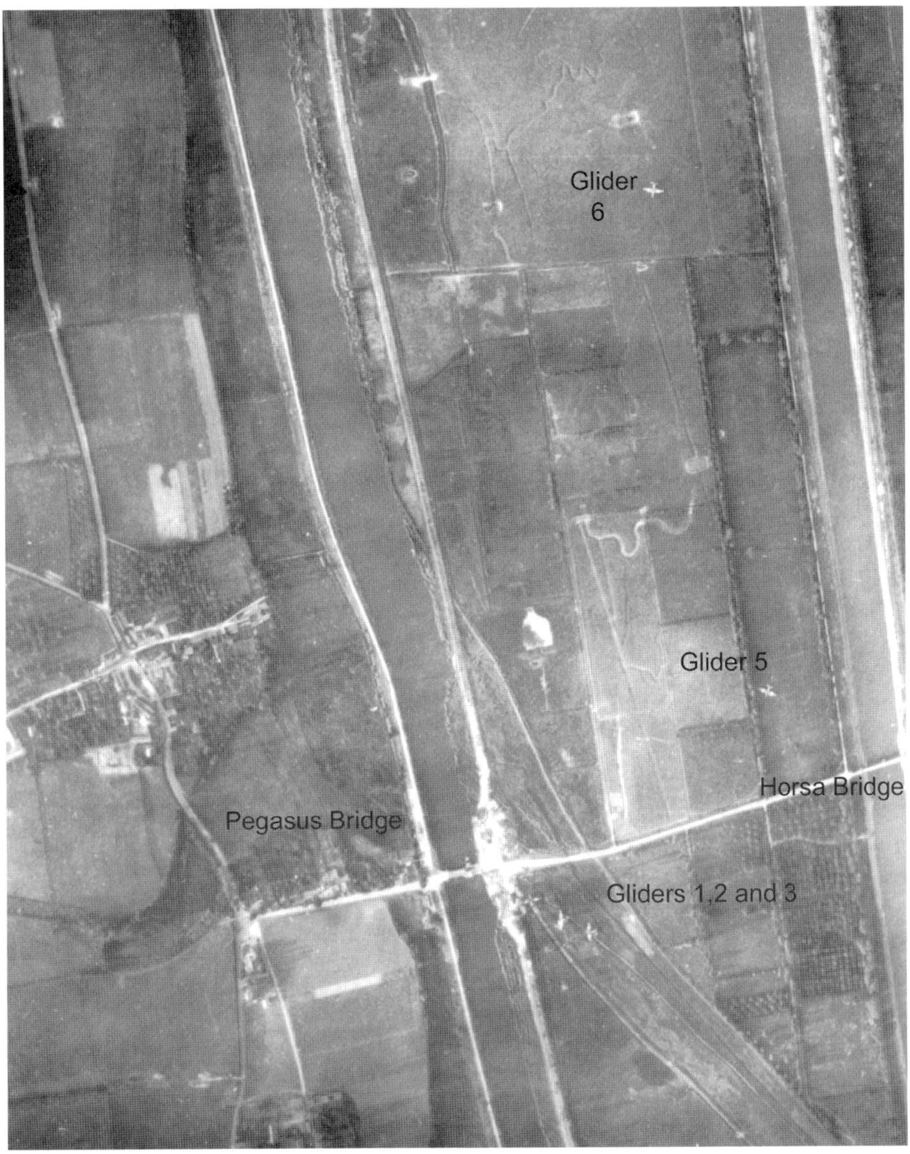

Pegasus Bridge and the Ranville Landing Zones.

British glider pilots after receiving awards at Buckingham Palace, December 1944. Left to right: Bruce Hobbs DFM, Stan Pearson DFM, W. Herbert DFM, Jim Wallwork DFM and Tommy Moore, MM. (GPRA)

risked breaking their legs as the cockpit smashed into the ground but decided the risk was worth it. As they had planned, the glider had come to rest within yards of its target, the impact so great that both pilots had been hurled through the windscreen with Ainsworth pinned under the wreckage. Jim Wallwork

> *went over headfirst and landed flat on my stomach. I was stunned, as was Ainsworth; I came around and he seemed to be in bad shape. I said, 'Can you crawl?' and he said 'No', and then I asked if I lifted, could he crawl out and he said 'I'll try.' I lifted the thing and I felt that I lifted the whole bloody glider when probably all I lifted was a small spar, but I felt like 30 men when I picked this thing up and he did manage to crawl out.*
>
> *'For a few seconds we sat, dazed and motionless,' John Howard later remembered, 'and then there was a mad scramble through the mangled doorways as the platoon went into action. For a moment I could see nothing and thought I was blinded, until I realized that in the crash my steel helmet had been rammed down over my face by the roof of the glider, so I came steaming out with an iron countenance! I must have looked incredible!'*

As his men attacked, Howard and his radio-operator Corporal Ted Tappenden set up his command post inside a trench near the perimeter wire.

Lieutenant Herbert Denham 'Den' Brotheridge and the men of 25 Platoon quietly moved into their assault formation. Brotheridge sent Corporal Jack Bailey with two men to deal with the bunker where their briefing had told them the firing mechanism to blow the bridges was located. Gathering the remainder of his platoon, he gave a whispered 'Come on lads' and led the dash for the bridge. Just one minute had passed since the first glider had landed.

As Staff Sergeant Oliver Bowland and Sergeant Philip Hobbs brought Glider 92 down within 25 yards of the wreckage of Wallwork's Glider 91, Lieutenant David Wood found himself thrown clear still clutching his Sten and a canvas bucket filled with grenades and, recovering quickly, gathered his men and headed towards the bridge. Shortly afterwards, Glider 93 arrived, crashing to a

THE FIRST CASUALTY

D-Day was a day of many 'firsts' as men vied to be the first to land, the first to capture a German or the first to liberate a Frenchwoman. One distinction was less sought after, however: being the first to die.

Edward Hull, a paratrooper in 9 Para, was hit by an accidental discharge at the transit camp near Broadwell on 5 June. He died the following day, arguably one of the first casualties of the operation. Later that day, as men of the 505th Parachute Infantry Regiment of the US 82nd Airborne Division boarded their aircraft, a Gammon grenade exploded, killing Robert Leakey, Pete Vah and Kenneth Vaught. All but one of the stick were wounded and another man, Eddie Meelburg, died later that night.

Lieutenant Herbert 'Den' Brotheridge, however, is generally regarded as being the first man to lose his life in action on D-Day. Hit in the neck during the attack on the Orne River bridge, he died about thirty minutes later, the first Allied soldier killed in action. By the time Brotheridge was hit, another member of the team, Lance Corporal Fred Greenhalgh, was already dead, thrown from his glider as it landed and drowned in a nearby pond.

The exact circumstances of Bombardier Hall's death have never been established, but his grave is unique in giving 5 June as his date of death.

A few yards away from Den Brotheridge's grave in Ranville churchyard lies that of another casualty. Bombardier Henry Hall, a 23-year-old member of the 53rd Worcestershire Yeomanry Airlanding Light Regiment of the Royal Artillery, was part of a glider-borne Forward Observation Group sent to act as fire controllers for the naval bombardment supporting the 6th Airborne Division. The precise details of his death are unknown, recorded simply as 'killed in action', but the date of his death is unique among the hundreds of graves nearby: 5 June.

In the chaos of the drop, it was impossible to keep track of every loss. Private William Richardson of 8 Para, for example, was hit and killed by flak during the flight to Normandy, his body returning in the Dakota in which he had travelled to Blakehill Farm airfield near Swindon. Others died as they jumped or plunged into flooded ditches, only to drown as they landed.

No-one is even certain of the true number that died on that first day, but estimates agree at around 2,500 men. In military terms this is a low figure for such a complex and large-scale operation, but each man's death was a major blow to the families who knew and loved them.

halt in the already crowded LZ 'X'. As it hit, the glider broke in half, throwing Lance Corporal Fred Greenhalgh into the nearby pond. Knocked unconscious, Greenhalgh drowned; the only casualty of the landing. Captain John Vaughan, the medical officer was also thrown clear and lay unconscious nearby. No. 14 Platoon's commander, Lieutenant Richard 'Sandy' Smith lay stunned and disorientated face down in the mud having lost his weapon in the crash. Quickly, though, the men recovered and raced to join Howard at the bridge.

By this time, Brotheridge and 25 Platoon were moving at a steady trot towards the two German sentries patrolling the middle of the bridge. Suddenly one of the sentries saw the British airborne soldiers now racing towards them and with a shout of '*Fallschirmjäger*!' turned and ran. The second sentry, a German NCO, pulled out a flare gun, but was cut down by a burst of fire from Private Billy Gray's Bren gun and a full magazine from Brotheridge's Sten. As he fell, the flare fired a warning into the sky just as Corporal Bailey and his two men tossed their grenades into the weapon slits of the bunker holding the detonators and followed them with a burst of fire. When the dust settled, there was no-one left to set off the charges. The first sentry had managed to reach the end of the bridge and had opened fire from a slit trench at the western end. The noise and ferocity of the attack encouraged some of the bridge's poorly-prepared garrison to seek employment elsewhere, but enough trained soldiers remained to react as Brotheridge continued his charge across the bridge. As he neared the far end, still running, he pulled a grenade from his pouch and hurled it into one of the occupied trenches. A machine-gunner in another enemy trench off to his right opened up and a round hit Brotheridge in the neck. Gray's Bren silenced the gun that had brought his commander down and 25 Platoon pulled the wounded Brotheridge into cover.

Two minutes after the first glider had touched down the first British troops had crossed the bridge and destroyed the detonators to prevent its demolition. Already, as Lieutenant Wood's 24 Platoon reached Howard, sappers were on the bridge looking for the demolition charges. They soon found that the intended sites for the charges were marked by paint, but that there were no explosives in place and the bridge was declared clear five minutes after landing.

Sandy Smith, his knee wrenched in the landing, hobbled after his platoon as they raced for the bridge. Reaching the far side, he saw a German soldier near the low wall in front of the Café Gondrée about to throw a stick grenade. A burst from his Sten killed the man, but the grenade landed nearby. Smith was trying to decide what to do next when one of his men asked if he was OK. It was only then that Smith saw the holes in his smock and trousers where the fragments of grenade had shredded his clothes and he realized his right wrist had been badly hit. Just then, he spotted a movement in a window of the nearby café and fired a burst. Luckily for the owner, Georges Gondrée, Smith's injuries had affected his aim. The shots went wide. Gondrée, awakened by the noise, quickly gathered up his family and headed for the cellar.

As 24 Platoon finished clearing their assigned trenches, David Wood, together with Sergeant Leather and a runner, made their way to Major Howard's command post (CP) to report their position clear. A burst of machine-gun fire wounded all three men and pinned them down. Immediately Corporal Goodbold took command of the platoon. It was now six minutes since the first glider had landed.

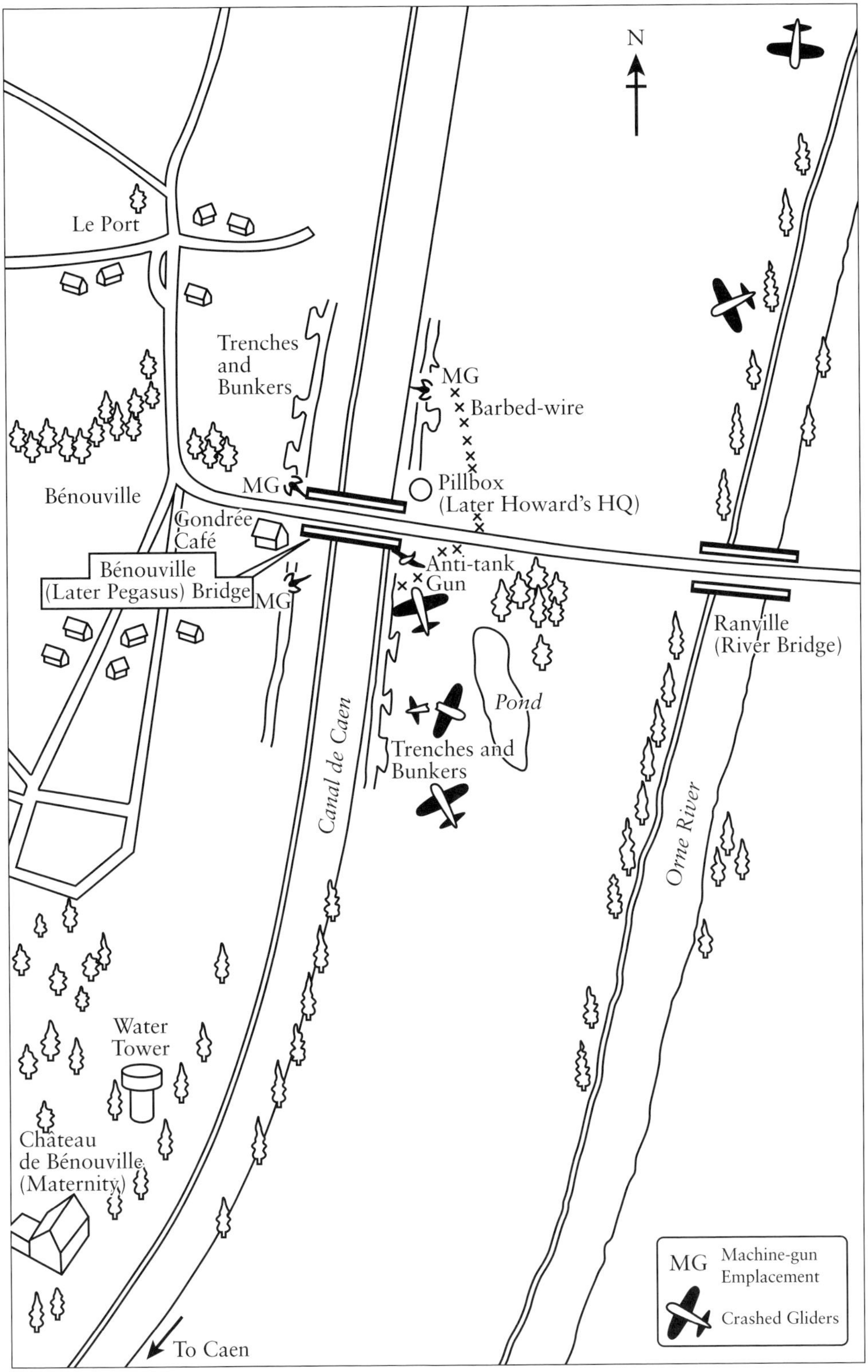

The Pegasus Bridge assault.

At the CP, Major Howard received the news that his friend Den Brotheridge was hit. 'It really shook me,' Howard said later, 'because it was Den and how much of a friend he was, and because my leading platoon was now without an officer. At the top of my mind was the fact that I knew Margaret, his wife, was expecting a baby almost any time.' Almost immediately, he heard that Wood was down and Smith wounded. With all three of his platoon commanders at the Bénouville Canal bridge injured, Howard was also worried that he had heard nothing from the Ranville River bridge.

AWARD CITATION

2572704 LANCE CORPORAL LAWRENCE GEORGE STACEY, NO. 23 PLATOON, 'D' COMPANY, 2ND BATTALION OXFORDSHIRE AND BUCKINGHAMSHIRE LIGHT INFANTRY

MILITARY MEDAL

During the coup de main operation starting 0020 hours 6th June 1944 on Benouville and Ranville Bridges, Lance Corporal Stacey gave an outstanding display of dash and initiative. On one occasion he captured an enemy staff car single-handed and successfully dealt with the three occupants. His fine example did much to inspire the men under his command throughout the whole operation.

A Horsa glider on tow.

The three gliders carrying Howard's men had landed exactly as planned, but those tasked with taking the river bridge were in difficulties. The gliders that had headed for the canal bridge had the relative luxury of a slow descent and were able to circle the target before landing. Those headed for the river bridge had to manage a straight descent by the shortest route. After casting off at 6,000ft, the Horsa could travel for around 12 miles at its usual rate of descent. Their target was only 5 miles away. Their LZ was a small field beside the river with a stand of 50ft tall trees at one end and a 40ft high embankment at the other. To hit either would be fatal. Beginning his steep 45-degree approach, Roy Howard, flying Glider 6, later described 'dropping like a streamlined brick'. Like all the gliders, his was overloaded and perhaps not simply with extra ammunition, for Howard was convinced that he also had a stowaway on board who was determined not to be left out of the action. Quickly, Howard ordered two men to the rear of the aircraft to try to balance the nose. It worked. Skimming the tops of the trees, Howard brought his glider in to the LZ, only to find a new and totally unexpected hazard. No one had mentioned the herd of cows grazing in the field. As the glider crashed to earth it hit one, shearing off the nose wheel and finally coming to rest just 6 yards from its intended spot and 100 yards from the bridge.

On the ground, Sergeant 'Wagger' Thornton gently reminded Lieutenant Dennis Fox that he needed to open the door and helped him as he struggled to

A Horsa on tow.

turn the handle. Once outside, 17 Platoon rapidly moved into formation with one section to the front followed by Lieutenant Fox, the remaining two sections and Sergeant Thornton bringing up the rear with the remainder of the platoon headquarters. When the lead section hesitated, Fox ran forward and was told by the section commander that there was a German manning a machine gun at the bridge. Fox told him to get his men moving, but when they still hesitated, Fox ordered them to start their approach. As they did so, the machine-gunner spotted them and opened fire. Thornton set up the platoon's 2in mortar and dropped a bomb directly onto the gun position. Seeing the mortar hit, Fox led his men at a charge, shouting their recognition sign 'Fox, Fox, Fox' as they ran. They reached the bridge just in time to see the last defenders run away as one of the lead section NCOs took over the abandoned MG 34 and sent a long burst after them. Contacting the canal group by radio, Fox informed them that only one glider had reached the bridge. Immediately, Captain Neilson led his sappers along the road and declared it safe just as Lieutenant Bence and his men arrived.

One minute after Fox's glider landed, Glider 95, piloted by Staff Sergeants Stan Pearson and Len Guthrie and carrying Lieutenant H.J. 'Todd' Sweeney's 23 Platoon touched down and came to a halt short of LZ 'Y' some 700 yards away from the bridge. Sweeney's men were climbing out of the glider as they heard the machine gun open up at the bridge. With Sweeney leading the way at the double, they raced for the bridge, only to fall victim to the deep drainage ditches along the edges of the field. Soaked and covered in mud, Sweeney led his men up to the bridge, confused by the lack of firing. Leaving one section to provide security, Sweeney went forward with the remainder of his men across the bridge at a sprint. As they reached the far end Sweeney spotted Dennis Fox and anxiously called out to him, 'Dennis, how are you, is everything all right?' 'Yes, I think so,' came the calm reply, 'but I can't find the bloody umpires!'

Leaving Fox to organize the immediate defence of the river bridge, Sweeney went across to the canal bridge to report to Major Howard. At 0026 hrs, ten minutes after Glider 91 had landed, John Howard had the news he had been waiting for: D Coy had successfully seized both bridges intact. Immediately Howard ordered Tappenden to broadcast the pre-arranged success signal – 'HAM and JAM' – and listened as his radio-operator repeated the message: 'Hello Four Dog, Hello Four Dog, Ham and Jam, Ham and Jam.' There was no response. Tappenden had no way of knowing that the radio carried by the paratroopers tuned to his frequency wasn't working. 'For a solid hour I lay on that road,' Tappenden recalled. 'I finally got so frustrated that I said "Hello Four Dog, Hello Four Dog, Ham and Jam, Ham and Bloody Jam, why don't you answer me?"' With the radio lost, no-one among the approaching 6th Airborne knew that Howard's force had captured the bridges intact.

At 0050 hrs, the small *coup de main* force heard the steady sound of aircraft engines and, in the light of searchlight beams and flak, saw the first landings of paratroopers around Ranville:

> *'We had a first-class view of the Division coming in,' Howard wrote later, 'Searchlights were lighting up the chutes and there was a bit of firing going on and you could see tracer bullets going up into the air as they floated down to the ground. It really was the most awe-inspiring sight. Above all, it meant that we were not alone.'*

THE ONE THAT WENT ASTRAY: THE STORY OF GLIDER NO. 4

Designated for the assault on the bridge over the Orne at Ranville, somewhere over Cabourg, the crew of Glider 4's tug had become disorientated as so many others would be that night. Casting off, pilots Staff Sergeants Lawrence and Shorter searched for any of the landmarks they had expected to guide them to their LZ. Spotting moonlight reflecting off water, Lawrence began his descent. 'We had a very comfortable, soft landing on the riverbank,' remembers Lance Corporal Clive, 'we got out and were only 50yds from the bridge and Captain Priday led the way.' Captain Priday and his men rushed the bridge, finding only one sentry on duty, who quickly decided the odds were against him and ran away, leaving his helmet hanging on the parapet. Looking around for anything he could recognize from the briefing models, Priday realized that they were in the wrong place. In fact, they had landed beside one of the River Dives bridges near the village of Harcourt, almost 20 miles off course, but for now Priday had no idea where he was. Quickly he sent Lieutenant Hooper and Staff Sergeant Shorter to a farmhouse nearby. Finding it empty, Shorter went back to report. Meanwhile, Priday split his force, deploying his men around each end of the bridge over the Dives. Soon after Shorter returned, a burst of German fire came from the direction of the farmhouse, hitting the wireless-operator in the head and killing him instantly. As the men stood to, Sergeant Raynor reported figures approaching. Thirteen soldiers around that end of the bridge flattened themselves into the grass along the bridge embankment.

Leading the group, the men saw the familiar figure of Lieutenant Hooper, hands raised, his boots tied around his neck, being pushed along by a German soldier who had a submachine gun pointed at his back with another escort walking further behind. Priday, Raynor and the two glider pilots quickly moved into position. As the group came within 10 yards, Priday shouted 'Jump, Tony!' and immediately opened fire as Hooper dived into the nearby ditch. As the Germans fell, the man with the submachine gun returned fire, cutting Priday's map case in half and hitting Sergeant Raynor's arm.

Throughout the rest of the night, the men of Glider 4 set up a defensive position and waited for dawn. As the day grew lighter, Corporal Clive saw a Frenchman with a young boy approach the bridge from the east and was able to confirm his location with them, as well as getting directions to their true objective.

After almost three hours of exhausting wading through flooded fields towards Robehomme, they found a farmhouse but, knowing that they were in the wrong place and would not be able to protect the family from German reprisals, the men avoided the farmhouse and instead settled into an outbuilding. Just as they began to relax, a large German motorcycle patrol arrived and parked their machines just 20 yards away. Priday decided that this was not the time to start his own war and the men lay low for two hours before the patrol left.

Finding their way to Robehomme, the small force collected scattered paratroopers from a variety of units and, following dry roads, were finally able to reach Ranville at around 0300 hrs on 7 June where a delighted Major Howard greeted Priday and his composite unit. The men of Glider 4 came in for some ribbing from their colleagues, but continued to argue that they had been sent to capture a bridge and that they had done just that.

As the men of the 5th Parachute Brigade hit the ground, they heard the faint sound of a whistle as Howard blew a signal to indicate that the bridge had been taken. The shrill sound, much to the annoyance of his men, carried for miles through the night air, but provided a useful encouragement to let the arriving paras know that the objective was taken and to help lost men find their bearings.

Five of the six gliders were down around the bridges, but Glider 4 carrying Howard's second-in-command Captain Priday and Lieutenant Hooper was missing, possibly meaning the loss of thirty men. Lieutenant Fox reported that 'I saw Brian Priday's tug and glider going off at an angle, and I thought the pilot was going to circle and come in', but the glider never arrived. Howard decided that the river bridge at Ranville was secure and concentrated his force around the Bénouville bridge, bringing Fox's platoon over to reinforce his men. As the platoon arrived, the sound of armoured vehicles could be heard, leading to a desperate search for the PIATs (Projector, Infantry, Anti-Tanks) that were still in the gliders. Most had been damaged in the landing and only one serviceable weapon could be found, which was swiftly set up by 6 Platoon in a forward position at the T-junction leading from Bénouville to Le Port from where it could command the approaches to the bridge.

Major Hans von Luck, commander of the 116th Regiment of the 21st Panzer Division, was the man expected to lead any counterattack east of the Orne, but he could not give the order to go. The convoluted chain of command prevented him from moving without orders, but Hitler was sleeping, as was Gerd von Rundstedt. Rommel was away from the area. Luck knew the importance of taking the bridges back, but was powerless to act on his own initiative. He decided to carry out a reconnaissance to determine the strength of the enemy around the two bridges and sent forward a small armoured column. If he found only a light force, he could contain them and recapture the crossings without deploying his forces fully. Hearing the sound of the armoured vehicles about an hour after they landed, the bridge defenders were vulnerable and knew it. Their only hope was to convince the Germans that this was a stronger force than it was. It was a single PIAT shot by Sergeant Thornton that achieved this. As the first vehicle to approach the bridge exploded, those behind withdrew, believing themselves to be up against a formidable force. Their miscalculation and hesitation meant that the bridges remained secure.

With two platoons now under the command of the wounded Smith, Howard's men were fully stretched in holding the bridge and patrolling the area, so it came as a great relief when, at around 0240 hrs, Howard was informed that 7 Para under Lieutenant Colonel Pine-Coffin ('Is that a code-name, sir?' Howard had been asked at the briefing) had arrived. Howard was able to pull his men back and, as he called them together, he was dismayed to find his losses meant that three platoons were now under the command of corporals. Redeploying into new positions, Howard was confident that dawn would greatly reduce the risk of a counterattack.

In the pre-dawn gloom, the men heard the naval bombardment offshore begin. Howard later recorded that

> *The barrage coming in was quite terrific. It was as though you could feel the whole ground shaking towards the coast, and this was going on like hell. Soon afterward it seemed to get nearer. Well they were obviously lifting the barrage further inland as our boats and craft came in, and it*

A bust of Major John Howard marks the landing site of his glider alongside Pegasus Bridge.

Major John Howard.

Pegasus Bridge.

Bomb damage caused by the air attack on the morning of 6 June 1944. A German bomb glanced off the bridge superstructure without causing serious damage.

A gun pit alongside Pegasus Bridge. It was from here that Private Wally Parr opened fire on sniper positions on the roof of the maternity hospital on the far bank.

The Café Gondrée, the first building to be liberated.

Mortar spatter marks where troops arriving from the beaches were caught as they tried to cross the exposed bridge.

Ranville Museum.

Lieutenant Colonel Otway bust at Merville.

The Merville Battery. A display marker on one of the casemates explains the story.

The crash site of Glider No. 4 at Varaville

Poterie de Bavant. This house became a hospital during the fighting of June-August 1944.

The Château St Come plaque. The château was held by 9 Para against determined enemy resistance.

The lane where Otway was wounded.

Bréville church.

Amfreville, the orientation table overlooking the landing zones.

The view from the high ground above Ranville shows why this area was so important. Any movement off SWORD Beach (to the right of the picture) could be observed from here.

Ranville churchyard; Lieutenant Brotheridge's grave.

was very easy, standing there and hearing all this going on and seeing all the smoke over in that direction, to realize what exactly was happening and keeping our fingers crossed for those poor buggers coming by sea. I was very pleased to be where I was, not with the seaborne chaps.

As the first troops began landing on SWORD Beach, Howard's men brought in two Italian prisoners – 'miserable little men, in civilian clothes, scantily dressed, very hungry' as Howard put it – ordered by the Germans to erect anti-glider poles on the landing zones next to the bridges and have them finished by dusk on 6 June. Howard ordered the men set free and made sure that they were given a forty-eight-hour ration pack. Certain that the Germans would be back to check on them, the Italians 'immediately went off towards the LZ, where they proceeded in putting up the poles. You can imagine the laughter that was caused all the way around to see these silly buggers putting up the poles.'

At about 0800 hrs, two Spitfires flew low over the bridges to see what was happening. Spotting Howard's ground signal indicating success, they put on a short display for the troops, flying over several times and performing victory rolls before one of the pilots dropped a bundle of early-morning editions of the papers. A short time later, Major General Gale, with Brigadiers Poett and Kindersley, casually strolled across from Ranville to congratulate Howard, ignoring the sniper fire directed their way. As they did so, two gunboats approached the Bénouville bridge from the direction of Ouistreham, firing on the bridge itself with a 20mm gun. As it came within range, men of 7 Para opened up with small arms and a PIAT, which scored a direct hit on the wheelhouse, causing the boat to ram into the canal bank. The crew surrendered rapidly, but the captain was more determined. Later, Howard described him as

an 18- or 19-year-old Nazi, very tall, spoke good English. He was ranting on in English about what a stupid thing it was for us to think of invading the Continent, and when his Führer got to hear about it that we would be driven back into the sea, and making the most insulting remarks, and I had the greatest difficulty stopping my chaps from getting hold of and lynching that bastard on the spot.

When Howard later sent him back to the newly-established PoW cage in Ranville for interrogation, the prisoner had to be 'gagged and frog-marched because he was so truculent and shouting away all through the time'.

Another attempt by the Germans to attack the bridge, this time by air, came at around 1000 hrs when a fighter-bomber roared along the canal and dropped its bomb directly on the bridge. The bomb failed to explode, but Howard was forced to acknowledge 'a wonderful shot...by that German pilot.' This was followed by a rocket attack by *Nebelwerfer* launchers. The 'Moaning Minnie' rockets were frighteningly accurate but failed to damage the bridge, instead prompting Private Wally Parr to use the heavy weapons sited at the bridge to fire on what he suspected were artillery spotters on the roof of a nearby maternity hospital, an action that local French civilians interpreted as a war crime by the retreating Germans.[2]

CHAPTER SEVEN

THE MERVILLE BATTERY

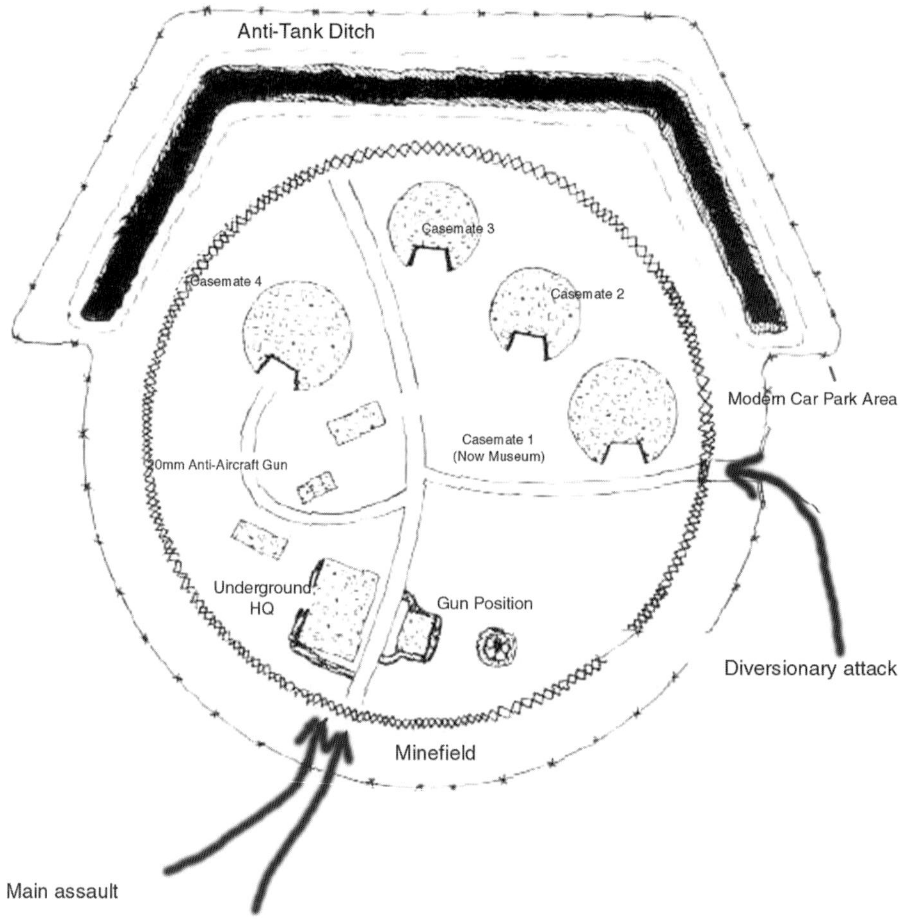

At 9 Para's final briefing in England, the RAF station commander wished the men luck and boasted that his men had never missed a DZ or failed to reach one on time. 'It was lucky for him,' one survivor said later, 'that there was no chance of any discussion on this point after the operation.' From the outset, the airborne assault encountered problems in the skies above Normandy. At 0045 hrs, the aircraft carrying the 540 men of the battalion's main body were just four minutes out from their DZ. Ahead of them the transport pilots were met by a huge dust cloud raised

by the bombing raid. The poor visibility caused difficulty in locating the DZ and pilots began their 'run-ins' at different altitudes and directions to those planned. The inexperienced pilots, already finding it hard to distinguish between the mouths of the Orne and the Dives, then misjudged the level of flak directed at them and began taking wild evasive action that put them even further off course. Behind them in the cramped fuselages, the heavily-laden paras were knocked off balance and many were still struggling to free themselves from piles of bodies and get back on their feet as the green lights came on to indicate that they had reached their DZ. Strong winds added to the chaos, and instead of landing in a concentrated rectangular area of some 1,900 x 800 yards, the battalion was spread over 50 square miles of Normandy, with one stick landing as far as 30 miles away from the battery.

Sixty years later, Lieutenant Colonel Otway told the London-based *Daily Telegraph* about that night. He never had the chance to jump and instead was blown from the Stirling bomber that had carried his men from Berkshire as flak hit it. 'It didn't kill anyone, but it blew a great big hole in the fuselage of the plane and certainly encouraged my men to get out of the plane fairly quickly,' he recalled. Only seven of the twenty men with him managed to jump over the designated DZ and the aircraft would eventually need four runs to drop everyone in more or less the right place. Off course and caught in the crosswinds, Otway found himself drifting

> *straight into the side of a building at first-floor level.... As if that wasn't bad enough, the building turned out to be one of the company HQs of a German regiment and after I slid down the side of the wall and looked up from the ground, this fellow popped his head out of his bedroom window and stared at me. Fortunately, one of my corporals had landed right next to me and he had the presence of mind to pick something up, probably a stone, and chuck it at the chap, who popped his head back in. Then we vanished and never heard any more from them.*

Lance Corporal Wilson, landing alongside Otway, had, in fact, landed on the roof of a glass hothouse in the garden of the farm, noisily crashing through it. The two men escaped and made their way to the RV.

On the ground, Otway found two very nasty surprises waiting for him. The area around the DZ was characterized by wide, water-filled ditches up to 10ft deep that surrounded every field and had either gone unnoticed by aerial reconnaissance or had simply been ignored. Either way, the men were not briefed about them and they were to prove extremely difficult to cross. To make matters worse, the Germans had opened the sluice gates of the nearby River Dives and flooded the fields over a wide area to the east of the DZ to a depth of around 4ft. Struggling through the flooded areas around the Dives, Otway recalled 'we saw several men who had been caught in the floods and were weighed down with their packs, just sinking. We tried to pull them out, but there was nothing we could do except watch them be sucked down by the mud. It was very unpleasant.' Scores of men remain missing, even to this day.

Reaching the RV safely, Otway waited for his men. By 0235, only 110 of the expected 750 had made it and the gliders carrying the heavy equipment, including the engineers with their mine-clearing equipment, the mortars, machine guns, anti-tank guns and medical support were all missing. By 0250, only another forty men had found the RV. To quote from Otway's official after-action report:

> *By 0250 hours the battalion had grown to one hundred and fifty strong with twenty lengths of Bangalore torpedo. Each company was approximately thirty strong. Enough signals to carry on – no three-inch mortars, one machine gun, one half of one sniping party, no 6-pounders, no jeeps or trailers or glider stores, no sappers, no field ambulance but six unit medical orderlies and no mine detectors – and one company commander missing. The commanding officer decided to advance immediately.*[1]

Otway surveyed his badly depleted force. With no heavy weapons, could 150 men armed mainly with Sten guns, rifles, grenades and knives take on an entrenched heavy artillery position whose defenders outnumbered the attackers? Weighing the damage the battery could cause on the beaches against the risk of losing the men he had with him, Otway said later that it was 'a question of moving off, or give up. In the Parachute Regiment giving up is not an option.' They set off on the ninety-minute march, with Otway adapting his plan as he walked.

The battery reconnaissance and rendezvous parties, meanwhile, had dropped on time and on location and immediately set out their lights and signals before the reconnaissance party moved out towards the battery, narrowly escaping the shower of 4,000lb bombs dropped by the Lancaster force. Not one of them hit the designated target, but a number of cattle in the nearby fields were killed and wounded, their terrified bellowing covering any noise the paras might make. Once at the battery, Major Smith was able to report that it was still active, but the garrison did not appear to suspect an attack was imminent. He was able to confirm the layout and strength of the battery and Otway used the information to modify his plan. The ground force would now have to destroy the battery with the limited explosives available to them. No mortar flares could be found and without these, the landing site for the gliders could not be illuminated and he could not rely on them being able to land on target.

Otway and his men moved into their start positions and waited for the gliders to arrive. Unknown to them, one of the three aircraft had been overloaded and its towrope broke before it left England. Its pilot, Staff Sergeant Arnold Baldwin, felt 'physically sick.... The passengers already knew that their big night was a flop....they were a very disconsolate unit as they disembarked.' The men were returned to Brize Norton and flew in another glider during the evening airlift. In the second glider, Private Gordon Newton of 9 Para had already had an anxious flight:

> *We knew that something was not right. The glider was 'crabbing' from side to side. We didn't realize what the problem was but the light went on and the co-pilot came through, very calm and collected and said, 'A knife please, any sort of knife, as long as it cuts.' I was sitting in the back seat. He said 'Just a minute mate', and pulled the back door open and cut the arrester gear off. We were about 10ft off the Channel.*[2]

Now, as they crossed the coast, the wooden Horsa glider filled with men and explosives shook as flak burst outside. Newton, flame-thrower strapped to his back, felt flak splinters hit his pack, fortunately damaging the air supply rather than the fuel tank.

The gliders and their tugs circled as they waited for a signal to guide them in. Under constant fire, the tug pilots gave the glider pilots the choice of either casting off or being towed back to England. They chose to cast off. As they did so, they realized that they were off target and heading for a village. Turning away, one crashed into a flooded field several miles away from their expected landing site in 3ft of water.

The third glider, flown by Staff Sergeant Dickie Kerr, was also under heavy ground fire but was at least on course. As they approached the battery, the aircraft was hit several times and four men wounded. Headed towards the casemates at 90 mph, the men braced for impact when another flak shell hit the tail, forcing the aircraft to swerve. As it sped towards a nearby field, the pilot saw a skull-and-crossbones minefield warning sign and pulled back on the stick, lifting it again and passing only feet above the men of the ground force before crashing into the orchard near the attack start line. Lieutenant Pond led his men out of the wrecked aircraft, by now missing both wings and on fire from where flak had ignited ammunition on board. As the men and their wounded comrades set foot on French soil, they realized that the Germans were approaching. A platoon of the 1st/736th Regiment of the 716th Division was approaching the battery to reinforce the garrison when Pond's men opened fire. The fire-fight lasted for four hours, but the German reinforcements were held.

As Otway watched the glider pass, he knew he could delay no longer and gave the signal for the gaps in the wire to be blown. The assault parties then moved against the battery, picking their way through the bomb craters, wire and mines on the way. With no mine-clearing equipment, the 'Trowbridge' party had cleared four lanes through the minefields with their bare hands, marking the paths by scraping the grass away with their boot heels. These paths were used to insert the few Bangalore torpedoes available.

Storming forward, firing from the hip, the paras charged towards the gaps in the wire. Unable to see the crudely-marked lanes, men strayed off the cleared

AWARD CITATION

4387903 CSM GEORGE DAVID MILLER, HEADQUARTERS COMPANY, 9TH PARACHUTE BATTALION

MILITARY MEDAL

Franceville Plage, 7th June 1944

This Warrant Officer was in Major Smith's reconnaissance party for the battery. By his initiative and courage he enabled Major Smith to produce a comprehensive report of the enemy defences. He then went on his own into enemy-occupied territory to assist Lieutenant Pond's glider without any thought of his own danger.

On the next day he was wounded, but returned to duty as soon as his wound was dressed and continued to fight until he was no longer able to stand and had to be evacuated, thereby showing a fine example of courage and determination.

paths onto the mines as the Germans fired flares and fought back fiercely, counterattacking from their bunkers. In a concrete shelter near Casemate 4, *Stabsfeldwebel* Büskotte contacted the battery commander *Oberleutnant* Raimund Steiner in the observation bunker overlooking the beach. Steiner then contacted another battery near Cabourg and requested that they fire on the perimeter of Merville.

Inside the wire, Otway directed the fighting from a concrete shelter. As he did so, a bullet passed through his water bottle and another through his smock. His men had begun to force their way into the bunkers, fighting hand to hand. Desperate to maintain the momentum of the assault, Otway committed his reserve to take on the machine-gun positions that continued to cause casualties among his men as they moved between the casemates. Under orders not to stop for casualties, the ground was soon littered with dead and dying men. Corporal Doug Tottle, one of only six medics to have reached the RV, followed the assault group:

> *My God, what a terrible sight. I thought I could stand anything like dead men, arms and legs blown off, men crying for their mums. I couldn't. It made me feel sick and I am sure I was. I then helped and did what I could with the aid of other medics.*[3]

Once inside the casemates, the paras found not the 150mm guns they were expecting but 100mm Czech howitzers. These were put out of action using explosives placed under the elevating mechanisms and the breech blocks. By now the fight had gone out of the German defenders and they began to surrender. The 150-strong attacking force was now down to 80 men still on their feet, but by then all but 22 of the German defenders were dead or wounded and of those survivors, only 6 were still fit enough to put up any kind of fight. As they took stock of their situation, Sergeant Eric Bedford commented to one of his men, 'Blimey Sid, here, take a look around. This is 9th Battalion, mate. Looks more like 9th Platoon to me.' Searching around the site, Bedford found the first German flag to be 'liberated' in the invasion in Casemate 1 and hastily stuffed it into his para smock.

Nearby, Corporal Tottle heard cries from Captain Hudson lying injured in the minefield:

> *Scared stiff, I ran through the minefield and did what I could for him. He was very badly wounded and I was unable to move him on my own. I looked up and the prisoners were being marched along the mine-free lane. I called out for some help and the corporal in charge ordered two of the Germans over to help me. They refused to walk through the minefield. This was soon sorted out by a few bursts of fire at their heels. With their help I managed to get Captain Hudson and a lot more of the lads out of the battery area.*

By then, about thirty casualties were being treated in the battalion aid post, hurriedly set up in a ruined barn close by. Twenty of them were stretcher cases. One officer had been killed and four wounded, and sixty-five other ranks killed, wounded or missing.

Among the walking wounded, Lieutenant Dennis Slade paused to remind Major Parry, who was also wounded, about the need to signal the ships. With no naval signallers or mortar flares, the only way to do this was either by use of smoke bombs in the hope that it would be seen and recognized, or by using the carrier pigeon that had sheltered throughout the attack under the battledress of Lieutenant James Loring, the signals officer. After circling the battery twice, the bird headed off in the wrong direction, arriving in England the following day. Cursing the traitorous nature of birds, the yellow smoke grenades were set off in the hope that spotter aircraft would see them. However, the gamble was too great and Otway ordered the evacuation of the site. Those too badly injured to be moved were left in the care of the medical officer Captain Watts, assisted by two orderlies and a captured German doctor.

The dazed survivors of 9 Para then made their way to the second RV point and moved off towards Amfreville. Behind them, a combat group of the German 736th Grenadier Regiment retook the Merville Battery and held it until the following day when two troops of 3 Commando once again fought a fierce battle in the casemates until the Germans were defeated. Almost immediately, German self-propelled guns counterattacked and drove the Commandos out, but by then the Merville Battery had been silenced and the threat to SWORD Beach was gone.

* * *

Back at the second RV, 65 of the 650 soldiers of 9 Para who had left England only hours before met with 7 Canadians of 1 Cdn Para at about 0800 hrs. Colonel Otway sat and wondered how to accomplish the rest of his mission with such a small force. Realizing that he could not accomplish the attack on the naval radar station at Sallenelles, he decided to head instead for the battalion's other task: the seizure of the high ground near Le Plein and Amfreville. They had not gone far before a Frenchman appeared to warn them that the little village of Hauger on their route was being held by around 200 enemy troops. By now it was full daylight and, after seizing the crossroads in front of the village, Otway called a halt. Yet again he was forced to change his plans at short notice and to bypass the village, heading now for the Château d'Amfreville, whose 6ft-high walls and loop-holed earth banks made a natural defensive position.

The château had been prepared for defence and was garrisoned by a force made up of Russians convinced by German propaganda that if they fell into the hands of the Allies, they would be shot as traitors. Their resistance was too much for Otway's tired men. By this point they had become so thin on the ground that there had to be an interval of 10 yards between each man simply to set up any sort of perimeter. There was no chance of them taking the château, so they set up positions around it to pin the garrison down, prevent any movement towards the Orne bridges and await the arrival of Lord Lovat's 4 Commando, by now fighting their way inland towards them.

CHAPTER EIGHT

THE BRIDGES

The overall role of the British 6th Airborne Division was to protect the left flank of the entire Allied assault on D-Day by denying the enemy the use of the ridge of high ground overlooking the Orne in the area between the Rivers Orne and Dives to the north of the road running from Troarn to Colombelles. If the British could secure and hold this vital ground by creating a barrier by destroying four bridges over the upper reaches of the Dives between Troarn and Robehomme, they would be able to delay any attempt by the Germans to send reinforcements towards Caen from the east and south-east. As the river turned away towards the north-east beyond Robehomme, it was decided that the demolition line should also include two smaller bridges over streams at Le Hoin and Varaville. The bridges had all been photographed by an RAF Typhoon fitted with a forward-facing oblique camera flying at just 600ft along the river and the photographs showed so much detail that Sapper Clark, a draughtsman at Headquarters Royal Engineers, was able to produce detailed scale models by which the demolition parties could be fully briefed and explosive charges calculated precisely. The task would fall to the sappers of 3 Parachute Squadron, Royal Engineers.[1]

The basic plan was that 3 Squadron (apart from its No. 3 Troop) would drop with 8 Para at 0050 hrs and would then proceed to the bridges at Troarn and Bures. There 1 Troop, protected by a company of 8 Para in the village of Sainte Samson and another in Troarn itself, would destroy the Troarn bridge, while 2 Troop destroyed the bridges at Bures covered by another 8 Para platoon. Meanwhile, 3 Troop would drop with 1 Cdn Para and destroy the bridges at Robehomme and Varaville. One company of the Canadian Battalion would cover the demolition at Varaville and a platoon would provide protection at Robehomme. Heavy equipment would land in three gliders with two of them carrying supplies for the main body of 3 Squadron and one for 3 Troop. Each would carry a jeep and two 10cwt trailers plus additional explosives and equipment. Without them, the sappers would have only hand trolleys dropped with them to carry the explosives needed. All the bridges were to be blown by 0715 hrs as the seaborne assault started, leaving only two hours for the attack on the Troarn bridge and, at best, three and a half hours at Varaville. In each case, it would involve an approach march of up to 4 miles in the dark with a heavy load of explosives and equipment and with the bare minimum of wheeled transport.

Varaville and Robehomme

The destruction of the small masonry arch bridges at Varaville and Robehomme had been assigned to 3 Troop under Captain Smith. It seemed a relatively straightforward operation but, like everyone else, the sappers experienced problems from the start as scattered jumps, lost containers and confusion put them behind schedule. Jumping north-west of Varaville with the Canadian Para Battalion, 3 Troop was widely scattered with some landing in the village itself and others across the flooded fields to the east with one stick, thrown to the floor by their pilot's attempts to avoid flak, dropped over a total distance of 3,500 yards. The containers dropped with them landed in 3ft of water, making them difficult to recover, even though they each had a lit location device attached. Despite this, Lieutenant Jack Inman managed to gather twelve sappers and find three of the explosives containers and between them carried the load over a network of ditches to Varaville to meet up with the lone figure of Lieutenant Ted Baillie. Baillie took charge of five sappers and 200lb of explosives and destroyed the Varaville bridges.

Meanwhile, Inman took the others and set off for Robehomme where the target was a steel lattice girder bridge 80ft long south-east of the village. On the way, Inman's group met up with Captain Smith, Lieutenant Beverley Holloway and three sappers who had all dropped further to the east. Smith decided that he would go on to the Varaville bridge and sent the others to Robehomme with Inman. Because the village of Bavent was garrisoned by German troops, the force made their way around it through the flooded fields carrying the explosives on their backs and eventually reached their target at 0900 hrs. There they found Sergeant Poole who told them that he had landed close to the bridge and so had already destroyed the steel span with a clean cut using 30lb of plastic explosive collected from the Canadians who had dropped nearby.

Bures and Troarn

Two 80ft-long steel lattice girder constructions at Bures – one a railway bridge, the other carrying a road – and a 110ft masonry road bridge at Troarn were the targets of the main body of 3 Para Squadron RE under Major J.C.A. 'Tim' Roseveare. The squadron should have dropped with 8 Para between the villages of Escoville and Touffréville, but landed east of the road from Le Mariquet to Escoville because the pathfinders of 22 Independent Parachute Company had themselves been dropped in the wrong place. Instead of the expected support of the whole of 8 Para, the engineers found just a few paratroopers but no officers. Finding their way to the RV, Roseveare discovered that enough explosive and demolition equipment was available from kit bags and container loads to attack the three bridges at Troarn and Bures, but that only six hand trolleys were available to move these heavy loads across country. Moving off at about 0230 hrs, the march quickly turned into an endurance test with sappers injured in the drop struggling to keep up. After some time, the party met up at a road junction with a group from 8 Para who also had a jeep and trailer filled with medical supplies. Commandeering the jeep, Roseveare had it reloaded with forty-five General Wade demolition charges for the Troarn bridge. Leaving the infantry to secure the junction, the engineers split up with Roseveare, Lieutenant David Breese and seven sappers climbing aboard the jeep and setting off for Troarn, while Captain

AWARD CITATION

MAJOR JOHN COUCH ADAMS ('TIM') ROSEVEARE, HEADQUARTERS, 3RD PARACHUTE SQUADRON, RE

DISTINGUISHED SERVICE ORDER

For conspicuous gallantry and devotion to duty. On the night of the 5th/6th June 1944, Major J.C.A. Roseveare was given the task of blowing up an important bridge at Troarn. He was dropped some five miles from his covering force, but he immediately gathered together a small force of Royal Engineers and some transport and made for his objective. Troarn was held by the enemy but, showing total disregard for his own safety and magnificent leadership, he pushed his way through under heavy enemy fire and captured the bridge which he then successfully blew.

Tom Juckes and the main body of the squadron loaded all the plastic explosive and cratering equipment that could be gathered onto the trolleys and set off for the two bridges at Bures.

After making their way through the Bois de Bures, Juckes and his men reached the two bridges at about 0630 hrs. Meeting no resistance, they set to work with

AWARD CITATION

CAPTAIN THOMAS ROLAND JUCKES, NO. 2 TROOP, 3RD PARACHUTE SQUADRON, RE

MILITARY CROSS

From the time he was dropped near Ranville on the night of 5th/6th June until 1800 hours on 8th June when his Troop was relieved in their defensive position, this officer has displayed the very highest powers of leadership, initiative and personal courage. He has been continually engaged in the execution of RE tasks in the face of the enemy and has led his Troop in an infantry role in a most aggressive fashion. After completing the demolition of two bridges at Bures he led a party including a platoon of 8th Para Battalion and forced a passage through Troarn, killing a number of Germans and taking prisoners and carried out further demolitions on the partially demolished Troarn bridge. On withdrawing to the Brigade area at Le Mesnil his Troop occupied defensive positions for 30 hours, inflicting heavy casualties on the enemy. During this time he supervised the laying of an anti-tank minefield under fire. Throughout the whole of this time he lost no opportunity in harassing the enemy. This officer set a magnificent example to his junior officers and men by his tireless energy, enthusiasm and offensive eagerness.

Lieutenant John Shave and a section of men tackling the farm track bridge, while Lieutenant Alan Forster and a reinforced section set their charges on the railway bridge. With no infantry available, the sappers of 1 Troop provided cover. After giving a local farmer a few minutes to move his cattle back across the river to the home side, both bridges were blown at about 0930 hrs and Captain Juckes led the men back to the RV with 8 Para by 1215 hrs.

AWARD CITATION

LIEUTENANT JOHN STANLEY RANNARD SHAVE, NO. 6 SECTION, NO. 2 TROOP, 3RD PARACHUTE SQUADRON, RE

MILITARY CROSS

This officer dropped at 0050 hours on 6th June near Ranville and was with the party that arrived at the Bures bridges. With his section he [managed] to make a successful demolition of the girder road bridge, cutting the span in two places with the minimum amount of explosives. In the subsequent attack on Troarn bridge Lieutenant Shave was in command of a protective detachment which covered the rear of the party into Troarn and their subsequent withdrawal on completion of the task. During 7th and 8th June Lieutenant Shave's section were in defensive positions in a forward area east of Le Mesnil. The enemy were very active in this sector and the positions were continuously under heavy shell and mortar fire. The courage and determination shown by Lieutenant Shave during this period had a great bearing on the successful defence in this area. At 1800 hours on 9th June Lieutenant Shave and his section were detached under command 8th Parachute Battalion in area 141704 for purpose of offensive patrolling in Bures and Troarn area. That night he led a small reconnaissance patrol of three other ranks to try to reach Troarn bridge. The patrol passed through the Bois de Bures and located an enemy patrol at the destroyed railway bridge. Moving south to the destroyed road bridge, Lieutenant Shave crossed the river and was challenged by some Germans. Lieutenant Shave replied with a 36 grenade killing two and the patrol returned to Battalion. On the night of the 11th/12th he again led a similar patrol to the same area. This time two sappers were left at the Bures railway bridge and Lieutenant Shave and Sapper Hurst crossed the river by the wrecked girders of the railway bridge and proceeded south towards Troarn bridge. An enemy patrol was encountered, however, and the bridge was not reached. The patrol returned safety in two parties of two. At 0630 hours on 13th June 2 platoons 8th Parachute Battalion and Lieutenant Shave's section attempted to crater road Bavent-Troarn but were met by fire causing casualties to infantry and had to retire. At 2230 hours that night 1 company and 1 platoon and the section RE went out with Commanding Officer 8th Battalion in command and successfully cratered the road and track 166715 with 80lb of PE and returned safely to Battalion. Throughout these many engagements with the enemy Lieutenant Shave's enthusiasm and offensive eagerness has been of a high order.

Meanwhile, Major Roseveare and his men had a very different experience. Leaving the infantry behind at the junction, Roseveare later reported:

> *We set off down the road at a moderate pace with everyone ready with a Bren gun or one of our several Sten guns for any trouble. Just before the level crossing we ran slap into a barbed-wire knife-rest roadblock. One Boche fired a shot and then went off. It took twenty minutes' hard work with wire cutters before the jeep was freed. We then proceeded on, leaving behind, it transpired later, Sapper Moon; two scouts were sent ahead to the next crossroads. As they arrived a Boche soldier cycled across complete with rifle. On being dragged from his bicycle he protested volubly and we made the mistake of silencing him with a Sten gun instead of a knife. The*

AWARD CITATION

LIEUTENANT GEORGE ANTHONY JOHNSON WADE, NO. 2 TROOP, 3RD PARACHUTE SQUADRON, RE

MILITARY CROSS

Since dropping near Ranville at 0050 hours on 6th June this officer has shown the most exceptional initiative, courage and leadership. Having reached the bridges at Bures with the main party of the Squadron he was sent on a reconnaissance and found a Jeep and trailer loaded with the special charges for the Troarn bridge. He at once attempted to reach the bridge with a small party but was unable to get through Troarn owing to the enemy. Later in the day Lieutenant Wade was able to reach the bridge on foot alone and found one span destroyed. On the results of this reconnaissance a party was organised under Captain Juckes including a platoon of 8th Parachute Battalion. Lieutenant Wade was able to reach the bridge with his Jeep and trailer covered by this party and successfully demolished a second span and destroyed two boats on the site. On completion of initial RE tasks, the whole Squadron was in defensive positions in the Le Mesnil area. On the night of 9th/10th June Lieutenant Wade led his section on a raid on Bavent covered by one section 1st Canadian Parachute Battalion. The town was penetrated and booby traps laid and considerable opposition was encountered and the party was split up in hand-to-hand fighting with grenades. The Germans were left in complete confusion and many casualties were inflicted; all the RE section returned unhurt. On 10th June Lieutenant Wade's section were in defensive position at road junction 134726. Some Germans penetrated to a house and attacked the position with grenades. Lieutenant Wade was blown over but immediately set about clearing the enemy from the position. The enemy escaped but left an MG 42 and ammunition behind. On 13th June Lieutenant Wade's section was moved up with another section with a weak Company of 1st Canadian Parachute Battalion to reinforce a difficult position in the area Chateau St Come 138740. Some of the hardest fighting in the area ensued including attacks by Mk IV tanks. Lieutenant Wade led his section with great courage and coolness during a very difficult time. This officer has been an outstanding example to all throughout the operation.

town [Troarn] was now getting roused so we lost no time and everyone jumped aboard while I tried to make the best speed possible. As the total load was about 3,000lb we only made about 35 mph. At the corner [of the town] the fun started, as there seemed to be a Boche in every doorway shooting like mad. However, the boys got to work with their Sten guns and Sapper Peachey did very good work as rear gunner with the Bren gun. What saved the day was the steep hill down the main street. As the speed rose rapidly we careered from side-to-side of the road, as the heavy trailer was swinging violently, we were chased out of the town by a German machine gun which fired tracer just over our heads. On arrival at the bridge which was not held, we found that Sapper Peachey and his Bren gun were missing. Thirty-nine General Wade charges were immediately placed across the centre span, a Cordtex [detonating cord] lead was connected up and the charges fired. The demolition was completely successful – the whole centre span being completely demolished giving a gap of 15 to 20ft. The time taken was about five minutes. I decided Troarn would not be a healthy spot to return to, so we drove the jeep up a track due north towards Bures as far as possible and then ditched it. It was now 0500 hrs. Lieutenant Breese made a reconnaissance of Bures which led him to believe it was occupied. The party therefore swam several streams south of Bures and took to the woods. A good deal of machine-gun fire from a road junction ahead made me alter my plan and I decided to make for Le Mesnil which was reached at 1300 hrs.

AWARD CITATION

SERGEANT SIDNEY DAVID SHRUBSOLE, NO. 2 TROOP, 3RD PARACHUTE SQUADRON, RE

MILITARY MEDAL

This NCO was in command of a protective detachment of sappers in the second attack on Troarn bridge during 6th June. After the infantry platoon had entered the town and were driving the enemy westwards, Sergeant Shrubsole led his party east towards the bridges. For half an hour he engaged the enemy, killing one and taking the remainder prisoners, making the way open for the working party to reach the bridge. During the night of 7th/8th June this NCO was in charge of a small detachment of Squadron HQ personnel detailed to lay a small Anti-Tank minefield and roadblock just east of Le Mesnil. 100 Mk V Anti-Tank mines were laid on a vital tank approach under considerable small-arms fire. The mines in the road being set in holes blown with small charges, Sergeant Shrubsole laid the... charges himself and personally fused every mine. The successful completion of this minefield under fire was very largely due to the complete disregard for his personal safety shown by this NCO. Throughout the operation he had shown great powers of leadership and his cheerfulness under difficult circumstances has been invaluable.

AWARD CITATION

274140 CAPTAIN DAVID JOHN TIBBS, ROYAL ARMY MEDICAL CORPS, ATTACHED TO 13TH PARACHUTE BATTALION AS REGIMENTAL MEDICAL OFFICER

MILITARY CROSS

On the 6th June 1944 at Ranville, Captain Tibbs was in charge of a party of twelve stretcher-bearers, with the task of clearing the Divisional Landing Zone and a Brigade Defence Zone.

At first the Defence Zone was subject to light Machine-Gun fire and later in the day the area was heavily sniped. In spite of this and the lack of cover, this party, under the personal leadership of Captain Tibbs, worked unceasingly until 1400 hours, when they had collected all casualties. During the eight hours the party sustained two killed and four wounded, but regardless of personal risk, Captain Tibbs completed his task.

Back at the RV, at around 1230 hrs, 8 Para's commanding officer decided that since nothing had been heard from Roseveare, a further attack should be made on the Troarn bridge but that he could only spare one infantry platoon under Lieutenant G. Brown as a protection party. Captain Juckes, who had only just returned to the RV, formed up a force to make the attack. Along with Brown's platoon, he assigned one of his NCOs, Sergeant Shrubsole, to lead a protection detachment and a rearguard of more sappers under Lieutenant Shave. The demolition would be carried out by Lieutenant Tony Wade with six sappers and using forty General Wade demolition charges carried in a jeep and trailer.

From Bures, the party travelled down a road leading south towards Troarn and established a firm base just outside the town with the demolition party and Lieutenant Shave's detachment. Lieutenant Brown's platoon pushed forward and started to force the Germans back up the town's main street, while Sergeant Shrubsole's RE detachment went forward into the town and worked their way down the hill towards the bridge, killing one German and capturing another five. With their way now clear, the demolition party drove the jeep and trailer to the bridge and laid their charges on the span next to the one already destroyed by Roseveare. With the charges blown, a 40ft gap had been blasted and the piers badly damaged. The party then withdrew and the rearguard reached the 8 Para area at around 1630 hrs that afternoon.

CHAPTER NINE

THE LANDING ZONES

Back at the Landing Zones, the engineers of 591 (Antrim) Parachute Squadron RE had just ninety minutes to clear two night strips before the gliders arrived at 0320 hrs. Two engineer reconnaissance parties were to drop at 0030 hrs to tape out the two strips, with the rest of the squadron dropping at 0100 hrs to prepare the landing strips. With 4 officers, 12 NCOs and 120 men from 13 Para to act as labour, a protection party from 12 Para and a detachment of the divisional signals to provide a link with the aircraft, there was a lot to be done.

In contrast to many of their colleagues the drop was successful, but one reconnaissance party under Lieutenant Pip Mitchley was dropped wide and did not arrive in time to carry out its task so the other party under Corporal Stoner reconnoitred and set out both strips, despite a shortage of tapes to mark the whole area. Then, when the two squadron HQ sticks containing the squadron commander and his second-in-command failed to appear at all, Captain Fergie Semple of 3 Troop took charge and got the available men working as planned.

The anti-glider poles turned out to be smaller and easier to move than expected, with only around half actually in position in the ground. In many cases the explosives were not needed, but at the northern end of the LZ they had been wired together with heavy-gauge wire and these took longer to move. Nevertheless, the two westerly strips were ready in good time. Unfortunately, the lighting of the strips by the Independent Parachute Company was poor due to the loss of some of their men and equipment and as a result the gliders came in from all directions, although fortunately losses of men and equipment were remarkably light. As soon as the first wave of gliders was down, work began to clear two more strips further east and these were ready by 0500 hrs.

Among those arriving at 0320 hrs was Lieutenant 'Gunner' Read and fifteen sappers of 286 Field Park Company RE (Airborne) in four gliders. Three of these gliders were each to carry a Clark bulldozer, one American tipper trailer, petrol and tools. The fourth glider was to carry a jeep and air compressor. Normally the weight limit for the gliders meant that the unit used light agricultural tractors with specially-designed bulldozer blades to clear landing strips, but earlier in the year Chindits operating in Burma had landed behind enemy lines and set up landing strips in the jungle using the glider-borne 'Clark Crawler Tractor', a small American-made bulldozer. When the Commander Royal Engineers visited his counterparts at the HQ United States Aviation Engineers in England and asked if he could have three of these machines, he was told that they would be available.

Two of the three gliders carrying them and the fourth with the jeep and air compressor landed as planned at 0325 hrs, but the remaining glider broke its tow rope over the Channel and crashed into the sea, killing the French-speaking Channel Islander operator Sergeant Rousseau. On the ground, the bulldozers proved difficult to unload and one broke the loading ramp but survived the drop to the ground. The glider carrying the other had shed its nose wheel during the landing and freeing the machine took some time, but both were working on their strips by 0445 hrs. For the next eight hours, under sniper, mortar and shellfire, they cleared glider debris and filled in holes so that the two easterly strips were fully prepared by 2100 hrs when the next wave of gliders was due to arrive.

One other engineer group jumped that night whose contribution is all but forgotten. The 6th Airborne Division Postal Unit Royal Engineers was formed in 1943 under the command of Captain J.C.G. Hine and, despite arguments that the 'posties' would have little to do during the actual assault phase, planners

Tanks link up with the airborne force after fighting their way inland from SWORD Beach.

decided that elements of the unit should drop with the assault forces. Three men would travel in by glider and three would parachute in with the troops to set up the first Field Post Office at Divisional Headquarters on D-Day itself. They would later be joined by twelve more men who would land by sea over the next few days.

Captain Hines was one of those landing by glider close to the Orne bridges:

> *Nearby, a glider went up in flames and another straddled a wall. It was as though all hell had been let loose and I thought, 'If ever I get out of this, I shall be lucky.' I wondered how my 'jumper' lads had fared. (Later I found to my dismay that one had been wounded in the leg and thigh and another in the backside.) I'd no idea where we were, but discovered afterwards that we had come down west of Ranville, and close to one of the bridges over the River Orne which had been seized earlier by men of the Division who had crash-landed in gliders right on target. It seemed to me at the time that the chances of getting a postal service started were about as good as those of winning the pools.*

Making his way to divisional headquarters, Hines was asked what kind of trip he had had and was casually told that the route he had followed to reach the HQ was under sniper fire and that 'seven or eight chaps' had already been hit. Immediately he began to reconsider his plan to set up a courier service between HQ and the beaches that morning:

> *A short time afterwards, one of my corporals turned up. He'd left the UK with a stock of stamps and some other postal equipment but had become parted from it in the shock of landing. Having reported in, he went back to the landing zone, and after a search which took some time, he came back with the missing items intact.*

As his men arrived, they established themselves in a nearby barn and alternated between there and slit trenches, but by D+1 outgoing mail was being collected and the following day the Airborne 'posties' unit managed to make their way to SWORD Beach where they contacted the Beach Group Army Post Office S698.

On 11 June, Hine's widowed mother received a delivery of Ranville butter wrapped in cabbage leaves and packed in an emergency ration tin.

CHAPTER TEN

THE PERIMETER

Individually and in groups, the scattered paratroopers went into action. Men jumping towards the ends of the sticks in particular found themselves facing the enemy as they landed and stories emerged of lucky escapes and vicious fighting all over the area. Sergeant Jones of the Royal Engineers was reported to have been captured but to have escaped after killing eight of his captors with their own weapons. Elsewhere, Sapper Thomas, wounded as he drifted down in his parachute, pulled out two grenades and hunted down the men who had fired at him.[1] Those who could evaded enemy patrols and made their way to their RVs and units. As dawn broke, thousands of men were still missing, but enough had arrived to form a loose perimeter and to hold off the probing attacks of the Germans. At around 1300 hrs, the defenders of the Orne bridge heard a strange, wailing noise growing louder and louder until, with Brigadier The Lord Lovat and Piper Bill Millin at their head, 6 Commando appeared, only minutes behind schedule. Millin's pipes were a signal that 1 Special Service Brigade was on its way, to be answered by a bugle call to indicate whether the bridge was secure or under attack. As he crossed, Lovat shook Howard's hand, declaring 'John, today history is being made.' The first link between the airborne and seaborne invasion had been made. That evening, the men watched as the glider-borne Operation MALLARD brought in the remainder of the division's heavy equipment and tanks into LZs already crowded with wrecked aircraft. Together, the paras and Marines dug in and prepared to hold the crucial flank at any cost and during the coming months, that cost would be high.

A Bofors gun loaded into a Hamilcar glider.

Relieved by the Commandos, 9 Para moved out again to take up a position in the Bois des Monts woods around the Château St Come. There, Otway heard on BBC radio about the success of his attack, but with additional losses during the day and only a few stragglers having caught up, his battalion remained at an effective strength of only ninety men. For the next five days, those few tried to hold back a fierce counterattack by SS units determined to dislodge the airborne men and fighting patrols from both sides continually prowled the thick hedgerows around the para positions. On one of these patrols, Lieutenant Dennis Slade entered the château to find evidence of recent German occupation. The Germans had left in a hurry and the paras helped themselves to souvenirs including a ceremonial sword and a substantial amount of cash (rumours put it at anything up to 150,000 francs. Orders were sent to Otway to ensure that this cash was handed over to headquarters, but instead it somehow found its way to the quartermaster and was used to buy fresh rations).[2]

As German attacks became more and more desperate – to the point of an attack by bicycle along the narrow country lane – the paras found themselves under intense pressure. Papers found on one enemy body after yet another failed attack showed that the Germans were under orders to take no airborne or Commando soldier alive, having been told by German propaganda that the British would kill any prisoners they might take. On 10 June, the battalion reached its maximum strength as yet more stragglers reached it. There were now 270 men in the battalion; well under half of what Otway's command should have had on its roll. Against them, the 346th Grenadier Division prepared to launch another massive counterattack with artillery and tanks. In a desperate attempt to stop them, naval gunfire was called in to within 500 yards of the paras' positions. As the Germans continued their advance, Lieutenant Slade was seen brandishing his souvenir sword and calling on the men to stand firm, which they did. At one point the Germans broke through, but were fought back using knives and bayonets, and German bodies were piling two or three deep in places.

Elsewhere, the fighting was equally fierce. With only 160 men of 12 Para in reserve, the line was broken at the crucial village of Bréville on 11 June. Thrown into the battle, 12 Para advanced with fixed bayonets and plugged the gap. By the time Bréville was secured, only nineteen men able to fight on were left. Facing them, the German 3rd/858th Regiment was reduced from 564 to 146 men in three days of fighting.

By 12 June, the Germans were running out of steam but launched yet another large attack with a battalion of infantry supported by tanks and self-propelled guns. Three hours of steady artillery and mortar fire was followed by an intense forty-five-minute barrage before the main attack began. Holding their ground but losing men, Otway contacted Brigadier Hill to tell him that he was not sure that his men could hold out this time. Knowing that the situation must be critical for Otway to admit this, Hill sent his only reserve – sixty men of 1 Cdn Para – to help and their counterattack relieved the pressure. That evening, Otway and his officers were out inspecting positions around the château when a shell landed among them. One man was killed and Otway, along with Lieutenant the Honourable Paul Greenway and another officer were all concussed. Several days later Otway allowed himself to be examined and was found unfit for further duty. He was sent back to recover, leaving fewer than 200 men of his battalion behind. Although the men of 9 Para were relieved at the Château St Come on the morning of 13 June, they were to have no let-up. They moved instead to Le Mesnil and remained in the front lines until the break-out from the beachheads in August.

On the evening of 6 June 1944, Howard handed over control of the bridges to the 2nd Battalion, Royal Warwickshire Regiment and led his *coup de main* party to rejoin the rest of 2/OBLI at Ranville. Finding the battalion proved to be more difficult than expected and Lieutenant Sweeney and his men, scouting ahead, moved towards Hérouvillette and Escoville for an hour before they met German resistance and were forced back to 'D' Company. As a result it was not until 0300 hrs that Battalion HQ was finally located. There, to his delight, Howard found his lost second-in-command Captain Brian Priday, Lieutenant Tony Hooper and most of 4 Platoon waiting for him after their adventures on landing at a bridge further east. As Priday cheerfully pointed out, they'd been sent to capture a bridge and indeed they had; not the right one, admittedly, but a bridge nevertheless.

The following morning, the Ox & Bucks advanced on Hérouvillette and captured it without a struggle before continuing on to the next village of Escoville. After coming under heavy fire and taking casualties from a concealed 88mm gun the company forced its way into the village and set up positions at its southern edge. Almost immediately they came under sustained artillery and small-arms fire. Howard set up his command post in a farm building at around 1100 hrs, 'then there was a zip and I was knocked out.' Seeing Howard with blood streaming down his face, his men were furious and set out to kill whoever had hit their commander. As radio-operator Corporal Tappenden put it: 'Every man in the Company admired Major Howard more than almost anyone else alive, because he was a man that if he couldn't do it, you couldn't do it, and you weren't asked to do it. We worshipped him and we wanted revenge.' Fortunately, it was not a serious wound and within half an hour Howard was conscious and back in command.

Heavy shelling had prevented the movement of anti-tank weapons into position and a determined German attack supported by armour forced the company back to Hérouvillette where, with the entire flank under severe pressure, Howard began to consider the outlook bleak. A combination of fatigue and the head wound contributed to a sense of pessimism that Howard only shook off when quietly threatened with evacuation back to England and away from his men.

As time drew on, they remained in position and Howard noted that 'The biggest problem I had was keeping up the morale of the troops, because we had always got the impression that we would be withdrawn from Normandy to come back and refit in the UK for another airborne operation.' Constant heavy shelling began to take its toll, even among the highly-disciplined and well-trained airborne and Marine forces, and Howard found men going, as he put it, 'bomb happy':

> *At first many of us tended to regard it as a form of cowardice and we were highly critical. I remember that I tended to take a very tough and almost unfeeling line about it. But after time, when we began to see some of our most courageous comrades going under, we soon changed*

our minds. We could see that it was a real sickness. Men would hide away and go berserk during bombardments, and they became petrified during attacks. They could not be used for patrols, or even sentry duty, and the only answer was to hand them over to the medical officer, who, once he was satisfied it was a genuine case, had the man evacuated as a casualty. It was pathetic to see good men go down.[3]

This was not a problem confined to Howard's men. For the vast majority of the troops landing in Normandy, this was their first taste of battle and they found the fighting in the bocage country far more difficult than had been anticipated. Losses were heavy, in some cases reaching levels not seen since the First World War. On 30 June 1944, for example, the commanding officer of the 6th Battalion of the Duke of Wellington's Regiment (6/DWR) reported on the breakdown of his unit. He had arrived on the evening of 26 June to find a unit that had taken 23 officers and 350 other ranks casualties in the previous two weeks. In the days following his arrival, three more officers were killed and he stated that

seventy-five per cent of the men react adversely to enemy shelling and are 'jumpy'...each time men are killed or wounded a number of men become casualties through shellshock or hysteria.... There is naturally no esprit de corps for those who are frightened (as we all are to one degree or another) to fall back on. I have twice had to stand at the end of a track and draw my revolver on retreating men.

Hearing of the report, Montgomery was furious, calling the officer 'defeatist' and the unit was disbanded.[4] If the experience of 6/DWR was the exception rather than the rule, it was fear of just this type of breakdown that forced commanders to leave the more elite units like the 6th Airborne and the Royal Marines in action long after they should have been relieved.

Ranville Cemetery, the last resting place of men of the 6th Airborne Division.

On 17 June, Howard was again wounded during a mortar bombardment when a bomb splinter set off a stockpile of grenades and fragments struck him in the back. Taken by jeep to an aid post, he was operated on and the fragments removed. As the operation ended, the post came under mortar fire and Howard found himself abandoned as staff took cover. Finding his driver, he asked to be taken back to 'D' Company because 'it's quieter there than it is here.' Unknown to Howard, an administrative error had led to his wife receiving notification not of a 'mortar' but a 'mortal' wound. Her letters to him, directed to the hospital he had just left, did not reach him. It took two weeks before the error was finally rectified.[5]

It would be almost three months – early September – by the time the survivors of 'D' Company 2/OBLI would finally be withdrawn from the line and could make their way via the artificial harbour at Arromanches to a ship that would take them home. By then, Howard was the only officer of the company fit for active service. Of his original NCOs all his sergeants were gone, along with almost all his corporals. Just forty men of the *coup de main* party remained.

By the time they returned from France, the units making up the 6th Airborne Division had all taken casualties, averaging 40 per cent of their strength. In three months of hard fighting, the division had officially lost 821 men killed, 2,709 wounded and 927 missing. Unofficially, though, the figure is thought to be higher. Lieutenant Colonel Otway later said, 'We were there and know the numbers, which Civil Servants do not. And we have been in touch with the families of missing men.'[6] To this day, the men of 9 Para alone claim that more than 190 of their comrades remain unaccounted for, lost in the flooded fields of France.

CHAPTER ELEVEN

EPILOGUE

In March 1945, men of 2/OBLI would again be sent to seize bridges, this time over the River IJssel as part of Operation VARSITY as the ground war reached Germany. The lessons of Normandy had been learned. This time the drops would take place in daylight. Adopting a new tactical approach, gliders would land not where remote planners thought they should, but where company commanders needed them. The hard-won and bloody lessons of Arnhem of September 1944 had also been learned. This time there would be no second and third waves spread out over hours or days: all the men would land together, a total of almost 22,000 British and American airborne troops dropped into an area just 5 miles deep and 6 miles wide in the most concentrated airborne assault ever attempted.

Glider-borne forces en route to the Rhine in Operation VARSITY, 1945.

At 0600 hrs on 24 March, the first aircraft carrying men of the 6th Airborne Division began to lift off and formed an air fleet over Essex, while the US 17th Airborne's aircraft lifted off from their French bases to rendezvous over the famous Belgian battlefield of Waterloo. By that time, the British gliders alone formed a stream that took forty minutes to pass overhead. Together, they began the 100-mile run to their targets. Some 4 to 6 miles east of the Rhine, the two streams formed a vast armada that would take two and a half hours to pass any given point. Even this armada amounted to only half the number requested, but it was by far the largest air operation of the war. Lieutenant Sydney St John, at 32 the 'old man' of the GPR, remembers that 'visibility was perfect and everywhere you looked there were tugs and gliders. It was extraordinary.' Earlier, at one of the many briefings and pep-talks the men had endured, a brigadier had exclaimed excitedly, 'won't those blighters be amazed when we cross the Rhine!' Looking around, St John couldn't help but feel that anyone would be amazed to find 1,300 gliders and hundreds of transport aircraft suddenly heading towards him in the largest airborne operation the world would ever see.

Out in front, leading the way, were the hardened veterans of Operation TONGA.

ENDNOTES

Chapter One

1. For details of the Garbo deception, see Juan Pujol with Nigel West, *Operation Garbo* (New York, Random House, 1985), or Roger Hesketh, *Fortitude: The D-Day Deception Campaign* (Wisconsin, Overlook Press, 1999).
2. *By Air to Battle* (HMSO, 1945), p.71.
3. Ibid, p.72.

Chapter Two

1. For a detailed account of the assault on Ében-Émael and the Albert bridges, see J. Mrazek, *The Fall of Ében-Émael* (New York, Presidio, 1970).
2. G. Devlin, *Paratrooper! The Saga of Parachute and Glider Combat Troops During World War II* (London, Robson Books, 1979), pp.22-23. See also W. Mitchell, *Memoirs of World War I* (New York, Random House, 1960), p.268.
3. Ronald Seth, *Lion with Blue Wings: The Story of the Glider Pilot Regiment 1942–1945* (London, Victor Gollancz, 1956).
4. Alexander Morrison, *Silent Invader: A Glider Pilot's Story of the Invasion of Europe in WWII* (Shrewsbury, Airlife, 1999).
5. Chatterton decided to 'stand by the men, despite the fact that I considered the plan mad'. His account of the operation was published in 1962 as *The Wings of Pegasus* (London, MacDonald).
6. Alastair Pearson in Max Arthur, *Forgotten Voices of the Second World War* (London, Ebury Press, 2004), pp.230-231.

Chapter Three

1. An extreme example of the problem is recorded by the historian Stephen Ambrose who reports the case of Lieutenant Robert Brewer of the US 101st Airborne at UTAH Beach who captured four Koreans. Originally conscripted into the Japanese army, they had been captured by the Russians in Manchuria before becoming *Wehrmacht* 'volunteers'. Elsewhere, Montgomery later wrote of 'Japanese and Turkish' prisoners in British hands. See Stephen Ambrose, *D-Day, June 6 1944: The Climactic Battle of World War II* (New York, Touchstone, 1995), p.34.
2. Ambrose, ibid., p.68.
3. Ibid., p.115.

Chapter Four

1. Details of this and other Royal Engineer activities can be found at the Royal Engineers Museum official website at http://www.remuseum.org.uk/index.htm
2. A fuller account of the selection and training of the *coup de main* force appears in Stephen Ambrose's *Pegasus Bridge: D-Day: The Daring British Airborne Raid* (New York, Simon & Schuster, 1985).
3. Two excellent accounts of the Merville operation are to be found in John Golley's *The Big Drop: The Guns of Merville, June 1944* (London, Jane's Publishing, 1982) and N. Barber, *The Day the Devils Dropped In: The 9th Parachute Battalion in Normandy – D-Day to D+6, The Merville Battery to the Château St Come* (Barnsley, Leo Cooper, 2002).

4. See H. St G. Saunders, *The Red Beret* (London, Michael Joseph, 1950).
5. Kevin Shannon & Stephen Wright, *One Night In June: The Story of Operation Tonga* (Airlife Publishing, 1994), p.31.
6. 'D-Day Veteran Reveals 62-Year Secret Before He Dies.' This story appeared in the *Wolverhampton Express and Star* and was reprinted in *The Eagle*, The Glider Pilot Regimental Association Journal, Vol. 11, No. 6, April 2007, p.11.

Chapter Five

1. Sir Hugh Wheldon, *Red Berets into Normandy* (Norwich, Jarrold Publications, 1982), p.3.
2. Ambrose, *D-Day* (op. cit.), Chapter 10.
3. Clark in P. Warner, *The D-Day Landings* (Barnsley, Pen & Sword, 2004), p.36. See also CSM Harries in Barber (op. cit.), p.43.
4. 'Do You Remember?' by 'A.B.' in *Pegasus: The Journal of the Airborne Forces*, Vol. 1, No.1, April 1946, p.21.

Chapter Six

1. Denis 'Eddie' Edwards, *The Devil's Own Luck: Pegasus Bridge to the Baltic 1944–45* (Barnsley, Pen & Sword, 2001).
2. For further details of the *coup de main* operation see Ambrose, *Pegasus Bridge*; Edwards, op. cit and John Howard, *The Pegasus Diaries: The Private Papers of Major John Howard DSO* (Barnsley, Pen & Sword Books, 2006).

Chapter Seven

1. *By Air to Battle*, p.83.
2. Barber, p.73.
3. Barber, p.93. See also Golley, p.119.

Chapter Eight

1. Details of the Royal Engineers operations can be found at the RE Museum's website at http://www.remuseum.org.uk/index.htm. See also J. Shave, *Go To It! The Story of the 3rd Parachute Squadron RE* (1948, but reprinted by The Airborne Engineers Association, 2003).

Chapter Ten

1. See http://www.remuseum.org.uk/index.htm
2. Details of these operations can be found in Barber (op. cit.) and Golley (op. cit.).
3. See Howard, *The Pegasus Diaries*, 2006, Chapter 11.
4. A full copy of the report is to be found at http://en.wikipedia.org/wiki/Duke_of_Wellington's_Regiment
5. See Howard, op. cit.
6. G. Devlin, *Paratrooper!*, p.403. See also Barber, p.202.

APPENDIX I

ORDER OF BATTLE

6th Airborne Division
Commanding General
Major General Richard N. Gale

Chief of Staff
Lt. Col. Shamus Hickie

GSO1 (OPS)
Lt. Col. Bobby Bray

GSO1 (AIR)
Lt. Col. Bill Bradish

GSO2 (OPS)
Major David Baird

GSO2 (Intelligence)
Major Gerry Lacoste

GSO3 (OPS)
Captain M.R. Spurling

GSO3 (AIR)
Captain Nick Pratt

GSO3 (Intelligence)
Captain J.H. Max

Glider Pilot Regiment
Brigadier George Chatterton

22nd Independent Para Coy
Major Francis
Gordon Lennox-Boyd

1st Canadian Parachute Bn
Lt. Col. George F.P. Bradbrooke

A Coy: Major D. Wilkins

B Coy: Major C. Fuller

C Coy: Major Hugh Murray McLeod

1st Wing
Lt. Col. Ian Murray

2nd Wing
Lt. Col. John Place

3 Parachute Brigade
Brigadier James Hill

8th Parachute Battalion
Col. Alistair S. Pearson
A Coy: Major Bob Flood
B Coy: ?
C Coy: Major John Shoppee

9th Parachute Battalion
Lt. Col. Terence Otway
A Coy: Major Allen Parry
B Coy: Captain Harold Bestley
C Coy: Major Ian Dyer

5 Parachute Brigade
Brigadier Nigel Poett

7th Parachute Battalion
Lt. Col. George Pine-Coffin
HQ Coy: Major Tullis
A Coy: Major Nigel Taylor
B Coy: Major Roger Neale
C Coy: Major R. Bartlett

12th Parachute Battalion
Lt. Col. Johnny A.P. Johnson
HQ Coy: Major George Winney
A Coy: Major Gerald Ritchie
B Coy: Major Harold Rogers
C Coy: Major C.W. Stephens

13th Parachute Battalion
Lt. Col. Peter Luard
HQ Coy: Major R.M. Tarrant
A Coy: Major J.F. Cramphorn
B Coy: Major G.W. Briston
C Coy: Major G.H.D. Ford

6 Airlanding Brigade
Brigadier the Honourable Hugh Kindersley

12/Devonshire Rgt
Lt. Col. Dick Stevens
A Coy: Major J. Roger
D Coy: Major John Bampfylde

2/OBLI
Lt. Col. Michael W. Roberts
A Coy: Major Gilbert Rahr
B Coy: Major J.S.R. Edmunds
C Coy: Major Johnny Granville
D Coy: Major John Howard

1/Royal Ulster Rifles
Lt. Col. Jack Carson
A Coy: Major Charles E. Vickery
B Coy: Major Gerald P. Rickcord
C Coy: Major F.R.A. Hynds
D Coy: Major A.J. Dyball

6th Airborne Div. Armoured Recce Rgt
Lt. Col. Godfrey R. Stuart

6th Airborne Div Signals
Lt. Col. D. Smallman-Tew

Royal Army Ordnance Corps
Lt. Col. J.L. Watson

6th Airborne Div. Ordnance Field Park
Major W.L. Taylor

Royal Army Medical Corps
Col. M. MacEwan

195 Airlanding Field Ambulance
Lt. Col. Bill Anderson

224 Para Field Ambulance
Lt. Col. D.H. Thompson

225 Para Field Ambulance
Lt. Col. Bruce Harvey

Royal Artillery
Lt. Col. Jack S.L. Norris

2 Airlanding Anti-Aircraft Bty
Major W.A.H. Rowat

3 Airlanding Anti-Tank Bty
Major Nick Cranmer

4 Airlanding Anti-Tank Bty
Major Peter Dixon

2 Forward Observation Unit
Major Harry Rice

53 Airlanding Regiment RA
Lt. Col. Tony Teacher

210 Airlanding Light Bty
Major the Honourable Charles Russel

211 Airlanding Light Bty RA
Major Jim Craigie

212 Airlanding Light Bty RA
Major Matt Gubbins

Royal Engineers
Lt. Col. Frank H. Lowman

3 Para Squadron RE
Major Tim Roseveare

591 Para Squadron RE
Major Andy Wood

249 Field Company RE
Major Sandy Rutherford

286 Field Park Coy RE
Major Jack Waters

APPENDIX II

OPERATION TITANIC

Operation TITANIC

German airborne commander Kurt Student had spoken of 'oil spot' landings where groups of paratroopers would be dropped in scattered areas and then slowly, like oil spots, expand towards each other. This, Student argued, would make it difficult for the enemy to identify the true goal and to react with enough force to prevent the incursion. Accidental scattering of airborne troops in Sicily and in the invasion of Burma had shown how much confusion had been caused by glider crashes far from their intended landing sites and how the enemy had tried to respond to dozens of reports from nervous sentries all across the area of operations. As D-Day drew closer, plans were drawn up to capitalize on the chaos of a night landing. At sea, Operations TAXABLE and GLIMMER would involve a feint towards Boulogne by ships of the invasion fleet while the Special Air Service (SAS) would be drafted in for the airborne diversion: Operation TITANIC.

TITANIC I

The first operation would be a simulation of a divisional airborne drop north of the River Seine to draw reinforcements from the south of the river back towards the Pas-de-Calais. Originally this was to have been undertaken by three teams from 2 SAS dropping in the area Yerville-Doudeville-Fauville-Yvetot, but this was cancelled on 24 May.

TITANIC II

This would aim to delay forces east of the River Dives from moving westward by dropping fifty dummy paratroopers fitted with flares and 'simulators' (firecracker-like devices to produce the sounds of rifle and machine-gun fire) in the Bois-de-Villers at H-4 hours and forty minutes.

TITANIC III

Troops south-west of Caen would be drawn away by another drop of dummy paratroops. Fifty would be dropped over Maltot and the wood north of Baron at the same time as the 6th Airborne Division began landing.

TITANIC IV

This, the largest operation, would involve a team each from A and B squadrons of 1 SAS. Lieutenant Noel Poole with Troopers Dawson and Saunders and Captain Harry

Fowles with Troopers Hurst and Merryweather would drop alongside 200 dummy paratroopers in the area of Marigny, about 8km from St Lo. Their job was to 'lend verisimilitude' to the drop of the dummies:

> *On landing they will remove the ballast, but leave packing materials, from any container they may find, in order that if the enemy find the empty containers (he) will assume that weapons and troops have been dropped.... They will then do anything in their power to make their presence felt, e.g. setting Hawkins mines on roads, shooting (Dispatch Riders), holding up solitary staff cars, etc.... On completion of these tasks, they will hide up. It is hoped to make special arrangements for evacuation by sea.*

Dropping to coincide with the first operations of the US 101st Airborne, the SAS, equipped with sound recordings of battle orders and gunfire, would 'create minor damage to culverts and will attack dispatch riders, lone vehicles, etc., allowing individual enemy to escape and thus confirm by personal contact the rumour of parachute-dropping.'

In 1940, the Germans had used straw-filled dummies during their invasion of the Low Countries to make their airborne assault seem even larger than it was. Later the same year, the British dropped decoy paratroopers near an Italian position at Siwa in North Africa as a diversion for a ground assault. By 1944, the tactic had been widely used. George Chatterton of the Glider Pilot Regiment had even suggested that 4ft-long model gliders could be used, but the idea was dropped as impractical. The dummies shown in the film *The Longest Day* depicted a fairly detailed model of a fully-equipped paratrooper, but in fact both the American version known as 'Oscar' – an inflatable rubber model for their operations – and the British 'Rupert' were far more crude efforts consisting, in Rupert's case, of a sandbag attached to a small parachute.

They were not the only strange objects falling from the sky that night. Brigadier James Hill, commander of 3 Parachute Brigade, had given his Canadian paratroopers a football with Hitler's face drawn on it in luminous paint. Prior to take-off, the ball had been returned to Hill, who promised to drop it in France. As his aircraft approached the DZ, Hill stood in the doorway and kicked the ball out into the night, quickly followed by 'three bricks, which they gave me with some rather vulgar wording painted on them' and which he had promised to drop on the German defenders. Even that paled into insignificance compared to the stuffed moose's head 'recruited' from an Exeter pub and dropped by Lieutenant Nick Archdale of 7 Para to 'put the fear of God into any German it hit'.

Operational Orders for the Decoy Plan – Operation TITANIC

Appendix B to SAS Brigade Operation Instruction No. 11 dated 19 May 1944:

1. Allocation of aircraft and loads:
   TITANIC I and IV 6 aircraft each carrying:
   39 dummies
   12 Pintail bombs

14 Rifle fire simulators Mk II
7 MG simulators (or rifle fire simulators if the MG simulators are not produced in time).

2. Descriptions of the various equipments are as below:

A. DUMMY PARATROOP
A model man made of sand-bags, approx 1/3rd the size of a normal man. Parachute to same scale.

B. PINTAIL BOMB
A small bomb containing a Verey light cartridge. It is released at the same time as the dummies, falls to the ground at a speed greater than that of the dummies and discharges a Verey light.

This serves three purposes:

i) Attracts enemy's attention to the area of the dummies' drop
ii) Illuminates the dummies in the air
iii) Makes it appear that there is a reception party on the ground signalling to the dummy dropping a/c.

C. SIMULATORS
These are mechanisms attached to the back of the dummies with a timed delay which is initiated when the dummy leaves the a/c. After the dummies have struck the ground, the simulators begin to explode.

They are made to represent rifle and LMG fire, and have a duration of approx. five minutes.

APPENDIX III

PEGASUS BRIDGE ASSAULT TEAMS

GLIDER No. 1
Objective: Canal Bridge

Wg Cdr Duder RAF, Tug Pilot

Staff Sergeant Wallwork, Horsa Pilot
Staff Sergeant Ainsworth, Horsa Co-Pilot

Major Howard, OC Coup de Main Force
Corporal Tappenden, W/T Operator, HQ D Coy, 2/OBLI

Lieutenant Brotheridge, OC 25 Pl, D Coy, 2/OBLI
Sergeant Ollis, 25 Pl, D Coy, 2/OBLI
Corporal Caine, 25 Pl, D Coy, 2/OBLI
Corporal Webb, 25 Pl, D Coy, 2/OBLI
Corporal Bailey, 25 Pl, D Coy, 2/OBLI
Lance Corporal Packwood, 25 Pl, D Coy, 2/OBLI
Lance Corporal Minns, 25 Pl, D Coy, 2/OBLI
Private Baalam, 25 Pl, D Coy, 2/OBLI
Private Bates, 25 Pl, D Coy, 2/OBLI
Private Bourlet, 25 Pl, D Coy, 2/OBLI
Private Chamberlain, 25 Pl, D Coy, 2/OBLI
Private Edwards, 25 Pl, D Coy, 2/OBLI
Private Gray, 25 Pl, D Coy, 2/OBLI
Private O'McDonnell, 25 Pl, D Coy, 2/OBLI
Private Parr, 25 Pl, D Coy, 2/OBLI
Private Tilbury, 25 Pl, D Coy, 2/OBLI
Private Watson, 25 Pl, D Coy, 2/OBLI
Private White, 25 Pl, D Coy, 2/OBLI
Private Windsor, 25 Pl, D Coy, 2/OBLI
Private Jackson, 08 25 Pl, D Coy, 2/OBLI

Corporal Watson, 2 Troop, 249 Field Coy, RE
Sapper Danson, 2 Troop, 249 Field Coy, RE
Sapper Ramsay, 2 Troop, 249 Field Coy, RE
Sapper Wheeler, 2 Troop, 249 Field Coy, RE
Sapper Yates, 2 Troop, 249 Field Coy, RE

GLIDER No. 2
Objective: Canal Bridge

WO Berry RAF, Tug Pilot

Staff Sergeant Boland, Pilot
Staff Sergeant Hobbs, Co-Pilot

Lieutenant Wood, OC 24 Pl, D Coy, 2/OBLI
Sergeant Leather, 24 Pl, D Coy, 2/OBLI
Corporal Godbold, 24 Pl, D Coy, 2/OBLI
Corporal Cowperthwaite, 24 Pl, D Coy, 2/OBLI
Corporal Ilsley, 24 Pl, D Coy, 2/OBLI
Lance Corporal Roberts, 24 Pl, D Coy, 2/OBLI
Lance Corporal Drew, 24 Pl, D Coy, 2/OBLI
Private Chatfield, 24 Pl, D Coy, 2/OBLI
Private Lewis, 24 Pl, D Coy, 2/OBLI
Private Cheesley, 24 Pl, D Coy, 2/OBLI
Private Waters, 24 Pl, D Coy, 2/OBLI
Private Clarke, 33 24 Pl, D Coy, 2/OBLI
Private Musty, 24 Pl, D Coy, 2/OBLI
Private Dancey, 24 Pl, D Coy, 2/OBLI
Private Harman, 24 Pl, D Coy, 2/OBLI
Private Warmington, 24 Pl, D Coy, 2/OBLI
Private Leonard, 24 Pl, D Coy, 2/OBLI
Private Weaver, 24 Pl, D Coy, 2/OBLI
Private Radford, 24 Pl, D Coy, 2/OBLI
Private Clarke, 48 24 Pl, D Coy, 2/OBLI
Private Pepperall, 24 Pl, D Coy, 2/OBLI
Private Malpas, 24 Pl, D Coy, 2/OBLI

Lance Corporal Harris, Royal Army Medical Corps

Acting Captain Neilson, 2 Troop, 249 Field Coy, RE
Sapper Conley, 2 Troop, 249 Field Coy, RE
Sapper Lockhart, 2 Troop, 249 Field Coy, RE
Sapper Shorey, 2 Troop, 249 Field Coy, RE
Sapper Haslett, 2 Troop, 249 Field Coy, RE

GLIDER No. 3
Objective: Canal Bridge

WO Herman RAF, Tug Pilot

Staff Sergeant Barkway, Pilot
Staff Sergeant Boyle, Co-Pilot

Lieutenant Smith, OC 14 Pl, B Coy, 2/OBLI
Sergeant Harrison, 14 Pl, B Coy, 2/OBLI

Corporal Higgs, 14 Pl, B Coy, 2/OBLI
Corporal Evans, 14 Pl, B Coy, 2/OBLI
Corporal Aris, 14 Pl, B Coy, 2/OBLI
Lance Corporal Madge, 14 Pl, B Coy, 2/OBLI
Lance Corporal Cohen, 14 Pl, B Coy, 2/OBLI
Lance Corporal Greenalgh, 14 Pl, B Coy, 2/OBLI
Private Wilson, 14 Pl, B Coy, 2/OBLI
Private Hook, 14 Pl, B Coy, 2/OBLI
Private Stewart, 14 Pl, B Coy, 2/OBLI
Private Keane, 14 Pl, B Coy, 2/OBLI
Private Noble, 14 Pl, B Coy, 2/OBLI
Private Crocker, 14 Pl, B Coy, 2/OBLI
Private Basham, 14 Pl, B Coy, 2/OBLI
Private Watts, 14 Pl, B Coy, 2/OBLI
Private Anton, 14 Pl, B Coy, 2/OBLI
Private Tibbs, 14 Pl, B Coy, 2/OBLI
Private Slade, 14 Pl, B Coy, 2/OBLI
Private Burns, 14 Pl, B Coy, 2/OBLI
Private Turner, 14 Pl, B Coy, 2/OBLI
Private Golden, 14 Pl, B Coy, 2/OBLI

Major Jacob-Vaughan, Medical Officer, RAMC

Lance Corporal Waring, 2 Troop, 249 Field Coy, RE
Sapper Clarke, 2 Troop, 249 Field Coy, RE
Sapper Fleming, 2 Troop, 249 Field Coy, RE
Sapper Green, 2 Troop, 249 Field Coy, RE
Sapper Preece, 2 Troop, 249 Field Coy, RE

GLIDER No. 4 (The one that went astray)

Objective: Orne River Bridge

FO Clapperton RAF, Tug Pilot

Staff Sergeant Lawrence, Horsa Pilot
Staff Sergeant Shorter, Horsa Co-Pilot

Captain Priday, 2 i/c D Coy, 2/OBLI
Lieutenant Hooper, OC 22 Pl, D Coy, 2/OBLI
Sergeant Barwick, 22 Pl, D Coy, 2/OBLI
Corporal Goodsir, 22 Pl, D Coy, 2/OBLI
Corporal Bateman, 22 Pl, D Coy, 2/OBLI
Lance Sergeant Rayner, 22 Pl, D Coy, 2/OBLI
Corporal Ambrose, 22 Pl, D Coy, 2/OBLI
Corporal Hunt, 22 Pl, D Coy, 2/OBLI
Private Allwood, 22 Pl, D Coy, 2/OBLI
Private Wilson, 22 Pl, D Coy, 2/OBLI
Private Hedges, 22 Pl, D Coy, 2/OBLI
Private Everett, 22 Pl, D Coy, 2/OBLI

Private St. Clair, 22 Pl, D Coy, 2/OBLI
Private Waite, 22 Pl, D Coy, 2/OBLI
Private Clive, 22 Pl, D Coy, 2/OBLI
Private Timms, 22 Pl, D Coy, 2/OBLI
Private Whitford, 22 Pl, D Coy, 2/OBLI
Private Johnson, 22 Pl, D Coy, 2/OBLI
Private Lathbury, 22 Pl, D Coy, 2/OBLI
Private Hammond, 22 Pl, D Coy, 2/OBLI
Private Gardner, 08 22 Pl, D Coy, 2/OBLI
Private Jeffrey, HQ, D Coy, 2/OBLI
Lance Corporal Lambley, Coy Clerk, D Coy, 2/OBLI

Sapper Brown, 2 Troop, 249 Field Coy, RE
Sapper Deighton, 2 Troop, 249 Field Coy, RE
Sapper Guest, 2 Troop, 249 Field Coy, RE
Sapper Paget, 2 Troop, 249 Field Coy, RE
Sapper Roberts, 2 Troop, 249 Field Coy, RE

GLIDER No. 5

Objective: Orne River Bridge

WO Bain RAF, Tug Pilot

Staff Sergeant Pearson, Pilot
Staff Sergeant Guthrie, Co-Pilot

Lieutenant Sweeney, OC 23 Pl, D Coy, 2/OBLI
Sergeant Gooch, 23 Pl, D Coy, 2/OBLI
Corporal Murton, 23 Pl, D Coy, 2/OBLI
Corporal Howard, 23 Pl, D Coy, 2/OBLI
Corporal Jennings, 23 Pl, D Coy, 2/OBLI
Lance Corporal Porter, 23 Pl, D Coy, 2/OBLI
Corporal Stacey, 23 Pl, D Coy, 2/OBLI
Private Allen, 23 Pl, D Coy, 2/OBLI
Private Bowden, 23 Pl, D Coy, 2/OBLI
Private Buller, 23 Pl, D Coy, 2/OBLI
Private Bright, 23 Pl, D Coy, 2/OBLI
Private Bleach, 23 Pl, D Coy, 2/OBLI
Private Clarke, 46 23 Pl, D Coy, 2/OBLI
Private Galbraith, 23 Pl, D Coy, 2/OBLI
Private Jackson, 59 23 Pl, D Coy, 2/OBLI
Private Roach, 23 Pl, D Coy, 2/OBLI
Private Roberts, 94 23 Pl, D Coy, 2/OBLI
Private Read, 23 Pl, D Coy, 2/OBLI
Private Tibbett, 23 Pl, D Coy, 2/OBLI
Private Wixon, 23 Pl, D Coy, 2/OBLI
Private Wood, 23 Pl, D Coy, 2/OBLI
Private Willcocks, 23 Pl, D Coy, 2/OBLI

Lieutenant Macdonald, 7 Para Liaison Officer

Corporal Straw, 2 Troop, 249 Field Coy, RE
Sapper Bradford, 2 Troop, 249 Field Coy, RE
Sapper Carter, 2 Troop, 249 Field Coy, RE
Sapper Field, 2 Troop, 249 Field Coy, RE
Sapper Wilkinson, 2 Troop, 249 Field Coy, RE

GLIDER No. 6
Objective: Orne River Bridge

FO Archibald RAF, Tug Pilot

Staff Sergeant Howard, Pilot
Staff Sergeant Baacke, Co-Pilot

Lieutenant Fox, OC 27 Pl, B Coy, 2/OBLI
Sergeant Thornton, 27 Pl, B Coy, 2/OBLI
Corporal Lally, 27 Pl, B Coy, 2/OBLI
Corporal Burns, 27 Pl, B Coy, 2/OBLI
Corporal Reynolds, 27 Pl, B Coy, 2/OBLI
Lance Corporal Loveday, 27 Pl, B Coy, 2/OBLI
Private Collett, 27 Pl, B Coy, 2/OBLI
Private Hubbert, 27 Pl, B Coy, 2/OBLI
Private Clare, 27 Pl, B Coy, 2/OBLI
Private Peverill, 27 Pl, B Coy, 2/OBLI
Private Pope, 27 Pl, B Coy, 2/OBLI
Private Whitehouse, 27 Pl, B Coy, 2/OBLI
Private Whitbread, 27 Pl, B Coy, 2/OBLI
Private Lawton, 27 Pl, B Coy, 2/OBLI
Private Rudge, 27 Pl, B Coy, 2/OBLI
Private O'Shaughnessy, 27 Pl, B Coy, 2/OBLI
Private Annetts, 27 Pl, B Coy, 2/OBLI
Private Summersby, 27 Pl, B Coy, 2/OBLI
Private Woods, 27 Pl, B Coy, 2/OBLI
Private Wyatt, 27 Pl, B Coy, 2/OBLI
Private Ward, 27 Pl, B Coy, 2/OBLI
Private Storr, 27 Pl, B Coy, 2/OBLI

Lance Corporal Lawson, RAMC

Lieutenant Bence, 2 Troop, 249 Field Coy, RE
Sapper Burns, 2 Troop, 249 Field Coy, RE
Sapper C.W. Larkin, 2 Troop, 249 Field Coy, RE
Sapper C.H. Larkin, 2 Troop, 249 Field Coy, RE
Sapper Maxted, 2 Troop, 249 Field Coy, RE

APPENDIX IV

OPERATIONAL ORDERS FOR THE PEGASUS BRIDGE ASSAULT

5 Para Bde 00 N. 1
Appx A Ref Maps 1/50,000 Sheets 7/F1, 7/F2, TOP SECRET1/25,000 Sheet No. 40/16 NW
To: Maj. R.J. Howard, 2 Oxf Bucks

INFM

1. The enemy
   (a) Static def in area of ops. Garrison of the two brs at BENOUVILLE 098748 and RANVILLE 104746 consists of about 50 men, armed with four LAA guns, probably 20mm, four to six LMG, one AA MG and possibly two A Tk guns of less 50mm cal. A concrete shelter is under constr, and the br will have been prepared for demolition. See ph enlargement A 21.
   (b) Mobile res in area of ops. One bn of 736 GR is in the area LEBISEY 0471 - BIEVILLE 0674 with probably 8 to 12 tks under cmds. This bn is either wholly or partially carried in MT and will have at least one coy standing by as an anti-airtpo picket. Bn HQ of the RIGHT coastal bn of 736 GR is in the area 065772. At least one pl will be available in this area as a fighting patrol, ready to move out at once to seek infm.
   (c) State of alertness. The large scale preparations necessary for the invasion of the Continent, the suitability of moon and tide will combine to produce a high state of alertness in the GERMAN def. The br grn may be standing to, and charges will have been laid in the demolition chambers.
   (d) Detailed infm on enemy def and res is available on demand from Div Int Summaries, air phs and models.

2. Own Tps
   (a) 5 Para Bde drops immediately NE of RANVILLE at H minus 4 hrs 30 mins, and moves forthwith to take up a def posn round the two brs.
   (b) 3 Para Bde drops at H minus 4 hrs 30 mins and is denying to the enemy the high wooded ground SOUTH of Le MESNIL 1472.

(c) 6 Airldg Bde is ldg NE of RANVILLE and WEST of BENOUVILLE at about H plus 12 hrs, and moves thence to a def posn in the area STE HONORINE LA CHARDONNERETTE 0971 - ESCOVILLE 1271.
(d) 3 Br Div is ldg WEST of OUISTREHAM 1079 at H hr with objective CAEN.

3. Ground
See available maps, air phs and models.

4. Intention
Your task is to seize intact the brs over R ORNE and canal at BENOUVILLE 098748 and RANVILLE 104746, and to hold them until relief by 7 Para Bn. If the brs are blown, you will est personnel ferries over both water obstacles as soon as possible.

METHOD
5. Composition of force

Comd Maj. R.J. HOWARD 2 OXF BUCKS
Tps D Coy 2 OXF BUCKS less sp Bren and 3" M dets. Two pls B coy 2 OXF BUCKS det of 20 Sprs 249 Fd Coy (Airborne) det 1 Wing Glider P Regt.

6. Flight plan

HORSA gliders available 6.
LZ X triangular fd 099745. 3 gliders.
LZ Y rectangular fd 104747. 3 gliders.
Timing. First ldg H minus 5 hrs

7. Gen Outline
(a) The capture of the brs will be a coup de main op depending largely on surprise, speed and dash for success.
(b) Provided the bulk of your force lands safely, you should have little difficulty in overcoming the known opposition on the brs.
(c) Your difficulties will arise in holding off an enemy counterattack on the brs, until you are relieved.

8. Possible enemy counter-attack
You must expect a counter-attack any time after H minus 4.
This attack may take the form of a Battle gp consisting of one coy inf in lorries, up to 8 tks and one or two guns mounted on lorries, or it may be a lorried inf coy alone, or inf on foot. The most likely line of approach for this force is down one of the rds leading from the WEST or SW, but a cross-country route cannot be ignored.

9. Org of def posn.
It is vital that the crossing places be held, and to do this you will secure a close brhead on the WEST bank, in addition to guarding the brs. The immediate def of the brs and of the WEST bank of the canal must be held at all costs.

10. Patrolling
You will harass and delay the deployment of the enemy counter-attack forces of 736 GR by offensive patrols covering all rd approaches from the WEST.

Patrols will remain mobile and offensive. Up to one third of your effective force may be used in this role. The remaining two thirds will be used for static def and immediate counter-attack.

11. Emp of RE
You will give to your Sprs the following tasks only, in order of priority: Neutralising the demolition mechanisms. Removing charges from demolition chambers. Establishing personnel ferries.

In your detailed planning of the op you will consult the CRE or RE comd nominated by him in the carrying out of these tasks by the RE personnel under your comd.

12. Relief estimate that your relief will NOT be completed until H minus 3 hrs, i.e. two hrs after your first ldg.
One coy 7 Para Bn will, however, be despatched to your assistance with the utmost possible speed after the ldg of the Bn. They should reach your posn by H minus 3 hrs 30 mins, and will come under your comd until arrival of OC 7 Para Bn as in para 13(b).

13. Intercomn.
You will arrange for an offr or senior NCO to meet CO of 7 Para Bn near their Bn RV at H minus 4 hrs 30 mins with the following infn: 1) are brs securely held? 2) are brs intact? 3) are you in contact with enemy, and if so where, and in what strength? 4) if brs are blown, state of ferries? 5) where is your coy HQ? In addition you will give pre-arranged sigs from the brs, to show that they are in your possession, about H minus 4 hrs 15 mins. OC 7 Para Bn will take over comd of the brhead and of your force on his arrival at the EAST br.

MISC
14. Gliders Loads
Gliders 1 - 4 one rifle pl less handcart. 5 Sprs. Gliders 5 - 6 one rifle pl less handcart. 5 men Coy HQ.

Detailed Load Tables will be worked out by you in conjunc with the RE and Bde Loading Offr.

15. Trg
The trg of your force will be regarded as a first priority matter. Demands for special stores and trg facilities will be sent in through your Bn HQ to HQ 6 Airldg Bde. Until further notice all orders and instrs to you on trg will either originate from or pass through HQ 6 Airldg Bde.

Both Bde HQ will give you every possible help.

NIGEL POETT, Brig. Comd. 5 Bde Para.

APPENDIX V

PEGASUS BRIDGE: A PERSONAL ACCOUNT

'Come on, boys. This is it!' – Memories of Pegasus Bridge

By Private Denis Edwards, 'D' Company, 2/OBLI
An extract from his memoir The Devil's Own Luck
(Pen & Sword, 2001), with permission.

The whole interior of the glider erupted into a hive of furious activity as everyone sought their various weapons and equipment. The exit door had been right beside my feet. Now there was only a mass of twisted wood and fabric across the doorway and we had to use the butts of our rifles to smash our way out. When it was my turn, I clambered out and dropped to the ground. I glanced around from beneath the glider's tilted wing and saw the canal bridge's massive steel superstructure towering above me. The pilots had done a fantastic job in bringing the slithering, bouncing and crippled glider to a halt with its nose buried into the canal bank and within 75yds of the bridge. As I moved forward I glanced back towards the glider and saw that the entire front had been smashed inwards, almost back to the wing...I had been very lucky, but I thought that those who were forward of me must have been badly smashed up or killed. There was no time to think about this, however. The medics would take care of the injured. A few of the lads were already up ahead and, not wishing to be left behind in this exposed place, I made haste to join them. Major Howard was already on the approach to the bridge and shouted, 'Come on, boys. This is it!'

Charging forward, we reached the wide steel bridge, letting fly with rifles and automatics, and threw grenades, shouting at the top of our voices to frighten the German defenders and to boost our own morale. An enemy machine gun on the far side of the bridge chattered into life. We returned fire and kept going, with our Platoon Commander Lieutenant Brotheridge leading the way. The machine gun was firing long bursts as we charged, and Brotheridge, who was at the very front of the charge, was hit and fell to the ground mortally wounded. Later, when we heard what had happened, every one of us was really distressed that Lieutenant Brotheridge should have been killed in that way at the very start of our mission. He was a man for whom we had the greatest respect. Like all our airborne officers, he had never asked us to do anything that he would not do himself. As we neared the far side of the bridge, still shouting, firing our weapons and lobbing hand grenades, the Germans jumped to their feet and ran for their lives, scattering in all directions. Relief, exhilaration, incredulity – I experienced all these feelings upon realizing that we had taken the bridge.

We expected the Paras to reach us within an hour and, with the bridges now in our hands, we had to defend them against whatever counter-attack might be made. Still operating to the detailed plan rehearsed at the briefings before our departure, we took up our prearranged defensive positions. Our seven-man section moved a short distance down to the west side of the canal and took up positions astride a single-track railway that ran from Ouistreham to Caen along the top of the embankment. We removed our heavy equipment and unstrapped our small lightweight entrenching tools. These had a short wooden shaft, with a metal head having a small pick and spade.... This was our only digging equipment; not the most effective tool, but just about the maximum that we could carry on top of everything else.... Apart from the scraping and chinking noise of our entrenching tools against the ballast stones, all was surprisingly quiet until the peace was suddenly interrupted by the sound of powerful engines from the west, somewhere around Bénouville. The accompanying clanking, rattling and squealing noises heralded the movement of tanks, and very obviously they were coming our way.

For tanks to arrive so quickly was terrifying and we stopped digging as they drew nearer. Our main concern was their size, as we had nothing to stop larger tanks. No doubt the guards who had fled from the bridge had been able to warn a nearby unit of our arrival and the tanks were sent to investigate. By now they were less than 50yds to my rear and moving towards the bridge. Suddenly I heard the familiar crack as one of the lads by the bridge fired a PIAT weapon.... We had all been trained to use these weapons and, frankly, we were thoroughly sceptical about their effectiveness against real tanks. To our utter amazement, however, within a second or so of the PIAT being fired there was a mighty explosion quickly followed by shouts and screams, and it was obvious that an effective hit had been scored on the leading tank.... The tank that was hit was a light machine, fortunately for us all, but still it burned very nicely, illuminating the bridge structure with a huge blaze of orange, red and yellow. There followed the sound of exploding ammunition as the tank 'brewed up'.

After the tanks were driven off we settled down to await the arrival of the Paras. All was quiet again until the parachute transports came overhead, when the German anti-aircraft guns and ground forces began firing into the night sky. The first few planes flew over with little opposition, but those that followed ran into heavy flak and at least one took a direct hit, was set on fire and came hurtling down like a comet from about 3,000ft. I couldn't see anything of them in the darkness but I hoped that the Paras and aircrew had been able to bail out before it crashed, since it hit the ground with such force that no one on board could possibly have survived the impact.... The Paras should have been with us within an hour but it was obvious from the way that they were being carried by the wind that they were being scattered over a wide area and not within the compact dropping zone that had been planned. The result of all the confusion was that it was around 0230 hours before the first of them arrived, and then only in dribs and drabs.

It became very tricky as figures suddenly appeared in the darkness. It was impossible to tell whether they were friend or foe until they got to within whispering distance and we challenged them with a pre-arranged password. We whispered 'V', and the correct response was 'for Victory'. A German patrol which came close to us was challenged, then cut down by the light machine-gun fire when they failed to respond with the password. Killed with them were three of our Paras whom they had taken prisoner, and who obviously had declined to supply the password at the appropriate time and so paid with their lives, along with the German patrol that had captured them. It was tragic bad luck, but a hazard of war.

Generally the night was quieter than we had expected, but with the dawn came Germans in droves and from all directions. Under cover of darkness their snipers had climbed into tall trees and buildings and from daylight onwards began firing their high-powered rifles with deadly accuracy. My first indication was the distant 'crack' as they fired and, almost instantaneously, one of our lads would crash to the ground. They were fantastic marksmen and seldom let off a shot without hitting what they were aiming at.... With no ammunition to spare we knew that there was no point in blazing away at every high tree and building in the surrounding area. In any event we were reluctant to disclose our defensive positions and firepower. We knew that the Germans could still have had little idea of our strength, so we were not keen to help them revise their estimates. All we could do was to lie doggo and keep a sharp eye open for a definite target. When we had to move it was a case of crawling rapidly across open spaces and, when we thought that we were reasonably concealed from view, jumping to our feet and running for dear life!

BIBLIOGRAPHY

Ambrose, Stephen, *D-Day June 6, 1944* (New York, Touchstone Books, 1995)

Ambrose, Stephen, *Pegasus Bridge* (New York, Pocket Books, 2003)

Edwards, Denis, *The Devil's Own Luck: Pegasus Bridge to the Baltic 1944–45* (Barnsley, Pen & Sword, 2001)

Golley, John, *The Big Drop: The Guns of Merville, June 1944* (London, Jane's, 1982)

By Air to Battle: The Official Account of the British Airborne Divisions (HMSO, 1945)

Lynch, Tim, *Silent Skies: The Glider War* (Barnsley, Pen & Sword, 2008)

Ramsey, Winston, *D-Day Then and Now*, Vol. 1 (After the Battle Publications, 1995)

Ryan, Cornelius, *The Longest Day* (New York, The Popular Library, 1959)

Shannon, Kevin & Wright, Stephen, *One Night in June: The Story of Operation Tonga* (Shrewsbury, Airlife, 1994)

Warner, Philip, *The D-Day Landings* (Barnsley, Pen & Sword, 2004)

INDEX

Ainsworth, Staff Sergeant John, 43
Airborne Forces School, 16
Aircraft, powered:
  Avro 504, 15
  Douglas C-47 Dakota, 21
  Vickers Vernon, 14
  see also gliders
Albert Canal, Belgium, 4, 11
Allied forces, 23
  Army Air Corps (1940s), 14, **17**
  1st Airborne Division, 16
  6th Airborne Division, 2–3, 21, **75**, 75–6
  6 Airlanding Brigade, 5, 8
  4 Commando, 61
  6 Commando, 72
  1st Battalion, Glider Pilot Regiment, 18
  1st Canadian Parachute Battalion, 33, 61–3
  2nd Oxford and Buckinghamshire Light Infantry, 4, **29**, 74–7
  6th Battalion, Duke of Wellington's Regiment, 75
  7th Parachute Battalion, 8, 28
  8th Parachute Battalion, 7, 62
  9th Parachute Battalion, 4, 56–61, 72–4
  12th Parachute Battalion, 8, 73
  13th Parachute Battalion, 8
  3 Parachute Squadron RE, 62–8
  22nd Independent Parachute Company, 33
  286 Field Park Company RE, 69
  591 (Antrim) Parachute Squadron RE, 37–8, 69
  Postal Unit RE, 6th Airborne Division, 70–1
Anti-glider poles, **24**, 25
Arethusa, HMS, 33
Atlantic Wall, 1–2, **2**, 22–5

Bailey, Corporal Jack, 46, 48
Baillie, Lieutenant Ted, 63
Baldwin, Staff Sergeant Arnold, 58
Bayerlein, General Fritz, 25
Beaufre, André, 14
Bedford, Sergeant Eric, 60
Bence, Lieutenant Jack, 28
Bénouville, 4, 7
  Bridge (*see* Pegasus Bridge)
Bofors gun, **72**
Bowland, Staff Sergeant Oliver, 46
Breese, Lieutenant David, 63
Brereton, Lieutenant General Lewis H., 13–14
'Broadmoor' (6th Airborne Division planning HQ), 2–3
Brotheridge, Lieutenant Herbert Denham 'Den', 46–8
Browning, Major General Frederick 'Boy', 16
Brown, Lieutenant G., 68
Bruneval raid, 16
Bures-sur-Dives bridge, 7, 62–3

Caen Canal, 4, 7
  see also Pegasus Bridge
Central Landing Establishment, RAF, 14–15, **17**
Chatterton, Lieutenant Colonel George, **18**, 18–20, 26
Chespaling, 28
Churchill, Winston, 12, 15–16
Clark, Lieutenant Colonel A. R., 42
Clark, Sapper, 63
Corinth Canal, Greece, 4
Counter-attacks, 55

Davies, Jim, 18
DEADSTICK, Operation, 26–30
Decoys, 22
Dives, River, 4
Divette, River, 7
Dogs, parachuting, 35

Down, Lieutenant Colonel (Airborne Forces School), 16
Dreme, Exercise, 34–5
Duder, Wing Commander D. H., 43
'Dungeon Party', Whitehall, 16

Ében-Émael, Fort, 4, 11–12, **12**, 18
Edwards, Private Denis, 94–6
Eisenhower, General Dwight D., 40–1
Equipment, personal, 42
Escoville, 63, 74
Exeter, training in, 30

Fallschirmjäger see Parachute forces, German
Festung Europa, 1–2
Feuchtinger, General Edgar, 25
FORTITUDE, Operation, 1
Fox, Lieutenant Dennis, 27, 52
Franklin, Benjamin, 10

Gale, Major General Richard, 9, 16, 26–8
Galien, Friar Joseph, 10
'Garbo' *see* Pujol, Juan
'G-B Force', 34
General Wade demolition charges, 63, 67–8
German forces:
- disposition 1944, **3**
- *Panzer Lehr* Division, 24–5
- 2nd Panzer Division, 24–5
- 12th SS Division, 23, 25
- 21st Panzer Division, 23, 25
- 91st Infantry Division, 25
- 116th Panzer Division, 23, 25
- 243rd Infantry Division, 25
- 346th Grenadier Division, 73
- 352nd Infantry Division, 25
- 709th Infantry Division, 22, 25
- 716th Infantry Division, 25, 59
- 6th Parachute Regiment, 22
- 736th Grenadier Regiment, 61
- 858th Regiment, 73
- *Luftwaffe*, 25
- parachute forces, **10–11**, 21

Gliders:
- Airspeed Horsa, 8, **19**, 35–6, **50**, 51, **51**
- DFS 230, 11
- GAL Hotspur, 15, **16**
- General Aircraft Hamilcar, 5, **5–6**, **37**, **41**, **72**
- Kirby Kite, **15**, 16
- previous operations, 4
- *see also* aircraft, powered

Glider Training Squadron, 15, 19
Gondrée, Georges, 48
Goodbold, Corporal, 48
Gordon-Brown, Captain, 34
Grant, Flight Lieutenant Tom, 26
Gray, Private Billy, 48
Greenhalgh, Lance Corporal Fred, 47–8
Greenway, Lieutenant Paul, 33, 73
Guderian, General Heinz, 23, 25
Guthrie, Staff Sergeant Len, 52
Gwinnett, Reverend J., 40

Hackett, General Sir John, 20
Hall, Bombardier Henry, 47
Harvey, Group Captain L. G., 14
Herbert, Staff Sergeant W., **46**
Hérouvillette, 74
Hill, Brigadier James, 9, 35
Hine, Captain J. C. G., 70
Hitler, Adolf, 1, **12**, 23–4
Hobbs, Sergeant Philip, 46
Hobbs, Staff Sergeant Bruce, **46**
Holloway, Lieutenant Beverley, 63
Hooper, Lieutenant Tony, 53–4, 74
Hopkinson, Brigadier George 'Hoppy', 16, 20
Howard, Major John, 4, 27, 30, 42, 50, 74–6
Howard, Staff Sergeant Roy, 51
Hull, Lance Corporal Edward, 41

Inman, Lieutenant Jack, 63
Iraq, 14

Jeavons, Lieutenant Stan, 38, **38**
Juckes, Captain Tom, 63–5
Jackson, Captain Tony, 33

Keeble, Sergeant Clem, 41–2
Kerr, Staff Sergeant Dickie, 59

Landing Zones, British, 7, **7**, **8**, 69-71
Leather, Sergeant, 48
Leigh-Mallory, Air Vice Marshal Trafford, 40
Lovat, Brigadier The Lord, 72
Luck, Colonel Hans von, 25, 54
Luftwaffe, 25

MALLARD, Operation, 5, 8
Marcks, General Erich, 25
Merville Battery, 4, 7, 30–4, **32**, 56–61
Meteorological forecast, 40
Miller, Company Sergeant Major George, 59
Miller, Flight Lieutenant Keith, 26
Millin, Piper Bill, 72
Millward, Fred, 33–4
Milston, Wiltshire, 2–3
Mitchell, General William 'Billy', 13–14
Mitchley, Lieutenant Pip, 69
Monte Vulture, 15
Montgomery, General Bernard, 14, 40
Moore, Staff Sergeant Tommy, **46**
Morrison, Alexander, 18
Musitano, Staff Sergeant Bill, 35

Neilson, Lieutenant Jock, 28
NEPTUNE, Operation, 4
Netheravon airfield, 26
Newton, Private Gordon, 58
Norman, Wing Commander Sir Nigel, 14, 20

'Oil spots', 12–13
Orne, River, 4, 7
Otway, Lieutenant Colonel Terence, 4, 30–1, 57–61, 73
OVERLORD, Operation, 4

Parachute forces:
  early, 13–15
  German, **10–11**, 21
  see also under Allied forces
Parachute School, Central Landing Establishment, 15
Parr, Private Wally, 55
Parry, Major Allan, 33
Pas-de-Calais, 1–2
Pearson, Staff Sergeant Stan, **46**, 52
Pegasus Bridge, 43–55, **44–5**, 94–6
  see also Caen Canal
Pine-Coffin, Lieutenant Colonel Richard, 54
Poett, Brigadier Nigel, 27
Poles, anti-glider, **24**, 25, 37–8, 69
Pond, Lieutenant Hugh, 34, 41, 59
Postal services, 70–1
Priday, Captain Brian, 53–4, 74
Prisoners, Italian, 55
Pujol, Juan, 1

Ranville, 7–8, 45, **45**, **75**
  Bridge, 50–5
  see also Pegasus Bridge
Read, Lieutenant 'Gunner', 69
Richardson, Private William, 47
Ringway (Manchester) Airport, 14
Robehomme bridge, 7, 62–3
Rock, Lieutenant Colonel John, 14, 18
Rommel, Field Marshal Erwin, 22–3
'Rommel's asparagus', **24**, 25
Roseveare Major John 'Tim', 63–4, 66–8
Rundstedt, Field Marshal Gerd von, 22–3

Saint-Aubin-d'Arquenay, 8
Schweppenburg, General Leo Geyr von, 22
SEA LION, Operation, 1
Shannon, Sergeant Bill, 34
Shave, Lieutenant John, 65, 68
Shrubsole, Sergeant Sidney, 67–8
Sicily airborne operation, 20–1
Slade, Lieutenant Dennis, 60
Smith, Captain Geoff, 63
Smith, Lieutenant General Walter, 40
Smith, Lieutenant Richard 'Sandy', 27, 48
Smith, Major George, 33
Stacey, Lance Corporal Lawrence, 50
Stagg, Group Captain J. M., 40
Steiner, *Oberleutnant* Raimund, 60
St John, Lieutenant Sydney, 78
Strange, Squadron Leader Louis, 14
Student, *Generalleutnant* Kurt, 12–13
Sweeney, Lieutenant H. J. 'Todd', 52

Tanks:
  allied, **70**
    M22, 5
    Tetrarch, 5, **6**
  German:
    Mk IV, 25
    Panther, 25
Tappenden, Corporal Ted, 46, 52
Tarrant Rushton airfield, 26
Tedder, Air Marshal Arthur, 40
Thornton, Sergeant 'Wagger', 51–2, 54
Tibbs, Captain David, 68
Toler, Major Ian, 26

Tottle, Corporal Doug, 60
Touffréville, 7
Tractor, Clark Crawler, 69
Troarn bridge, 7, 62–8
'Trowbridge' groups (Merville assault), 33

Varaville bridge, 7, 42, 62
VARSITY, Operation, **77**, 77–8
Vaughan, Captain John, 48

Wade, Lieutenant Tony, 66, 68
Wallwork, Staff Sergeant Jim, 26–7, 30, 43, **46**
Weldon, Captain Huw, 39
Wenzel, Sergeant Major, 11
West Woodhay, training at, 31
Wilson, Lance Corporal, 57
Witzig, *Leutnant* Rudolf, 11
Wood, Lieutenant David, 46, 48